A THOUSAND LITTLE
light BULBS

How to kickstart
a culture of innovation
in your organisation

Simon Banks

"Simon Banks is a man passionate about a topic critical to Australia's future: people and creativity. How grateful can we be that he has taken his wealth of knowledge and condensed it in an easy-to-read book that is fun, cuts to the chase and contributes in a thousand little ways. The 'answer' may be rarely that simple, but Simon leads the way to finding it and I would recommend this book to anyone at any level. It is a superb read."

Louise Mahler, Leadership Influencer, International Keynote speaker, Author and Coach

"Simon's book is so much more than a thousand little lightbulbs. He brings his signature spark and energy to awaken business leaders. This book is a manifesto for thinking differently. His expert innovation advice serves as a call to action. With this book, you can unlock your creativity today."

Mike Parsons, Award Winning Innovation Expert, Podcaster, Chief Innovation Officer – QUALITANCE

"*A Thousand Little Lightbulbs* is an insightful commentary on the 'why?', 'how?' and 'what?' of innovation. Simon's book is artfully crafted, well researched, easy to read and practical. The mantra of people, people and people and the innovation framework are two key takeaways from his text."

Dr Stephen Brown, International Leadership Expert, Strategist, Policy Advisor, Specialist in Change Management and Organisational Development, Experienced CEO and Executive

"Simon Banks has given us the shake-up we need to stop thinking about innovation as something done by people in the funky part of the office using design tools. This is genuinely fresh thinking about how businesses prepare themselves for the future by unleashing the imaginations of their workforces. It's transformational, for individuals and companies, because it reframes the process of innovation to address the fundamental barrier – the Ogre within telling us 'no'. Feel the creativity return as a thousand little lightbulbs go off in your brain from page one to the first step you take down the innovation highway. Enjoy!"

Jemma Enright, Innovation Consultant, Entrepreneur, Startup Coach and Angel Investor

"It's not often you get to read a book that entertains as well as gives you fresh insights along with a framework. Simon has written a book that tackles the emotional aspects and skillsets that make innovation something everyone can do – and what makes it engaging is the style it's written in. This book paints a very clear statistical set of reasons why my business needs innovation NOW. I have learnt how I can slay innovation Ogres, it's given my cat a purpose and is choc full of innovation tools. Simon illustrates with countless examples of great Aussie mindsets of how to make innovation feasible and achievable – no matter how you rate your creativity."

Brad Waldron, Author of *How to Present Naked*, CEO, Leading World Class Speaker and Facilitator

What people are saying

Since first publishing this book in 2018, there have been a few changes…

COVID has turned the world upside down as we knew it and has changed the way we look at almost everything.

Whilst that event is not mentioned in these pages, our very human traits of creativity and curiosity and our ability to reimagine and redesign the world we want to be part of has never been more important; individually or within organisations.

I know that the content in this book will be a very handy guide to help you on that path.

Happy days,

Simon

Acknow

S – Inspiration, determination and smile

R, L, E – Humour and never ending spontaneity

G, BD, R – For big conversations about the world, art and quirky things

J, J – All your good stuff

M, R, A, D – For truly stoking my creative fire

T'n'T – Making the nonsensical sensible with a grin

To **all friends** who have inspired me greatly by taking a path less travelled

First published in 2018 by Simon Banks
Reprinted in June 2021 and April 2022

© Simon Banks 2018
The moral rights of the author have been asserted

National Library of Australia Cataloguing-in-Publication entry:

Creator: Banks, Simon, author.
Title: A thousand little lightbulbs / Simon Banks.
ISBN: 9781925648386 (paperback)
Subjects: Creative ability in business.
Success in business.

Project management and text design by Publish Central
Cover design by Julia Kuris
Edited by Tamara Protassow Adams and Tanja Gardner of Team T'n'T Editing

Disclaimer

Contents

"Business as Usual" is *not* the new normal

Have you noticed that things in the business world are a little different? And by "a little different", I really mean "a whole lot different".

Business as Usual is not the new normal.

Things aren't just changing. They're changing rapidly. Disruption is everywhere. We're either sitting in the middle of one of the most exciting times in history for the business world, or sitting in a state of panic.

I like to agree with a recent Prime Minister who said that there's never been a more exciting time to be alive.

It's obvious to anyone who breathes – or at least, anyone who's paying attention – that the behaviour and thinking that worked in the old world (way, way back five or ten years ago) probably won't work in this new developing landscape and the possibilities that exist within it.

If you're a leader within an organisation, this is where the questions start to kick in:

~ Will we be relevant?

~ Can we deliver what our market is wanting?

~ Can we change quickly and be responsive?

~ Do we have the right people?

~ Will some smartarse startup steal our market share?

And at this stage, you'll probably find that one of two things kicks in: either more panic or more excitement.

The great news is that wherever you are on the panic/excitement barometer, whether you know it or not, you're designed to embrace ALL the possibilities in front of you.

Human beings are hardwired to smash it in this new business world. Making that happen, however, will require some interaction with innovation – along with its wingmen: creativity, imagination and curiosity.

So if you find yourself at the panicky end of the panic/excitement barometer, don't worry. That panic is very normal. Take a few breaths, grab a coffee, and just chill as you read through this book: it will help you to embrace that panic and kick some new world arse.

The great news is that embracing the world of innovation isn't as hard as you might think. Developing a workplace culture of innovation where you constantly have great ideas, services, products, and results is achievable. Simply making small shifts away from what you're doing now can produce big results.

For example, imagine that you're about to set off on a very long journey, just for fun. It's an old-school journey – before cars, so you're walking. (Well, OK, you can ride a horse if that works for you.)

You set off from your starting point in a dead straight line, just to see where you end up. After a day or two, you realise that the way you're walking is boring. You think long and hard about this, and wonder what to do. You know that a dead straight line is what you had in mind and what most people do; but this is pretty bland. The initial joy of your journey is disappearing.

So, you pivot five steps to the left, and head off in a slightly different direction. Just five steps. At first, you're still close to the relatively boring landscape you (and the horse, if you chose to ride one) started off walking through.

But gradually, things begin to change.

It's just small differences at first, but then you start noticing plenty more. The landscape is much more interesting now. There are beautiful trees. There are more people about. Food stalls are appearing… and is that live music you hear?

That small change in direction has created a big difference over time. So many more interesting things are happening now.

You're so glad you decided to shift direction. You didn't need to make any further effort – just that initial small change. A small step is often all it takes to start off down the innovation highway. Even the smallest shift can create a huge difference.

Yes, it really can be that simple.

Fresh thinking and innovation can just start with taking small steps in a slightly different direction. That may sound hard to believe. After all, innovation can seem so daunting. It can seem like something that other people do – other people who are much more talented than you.

Believe me, it's not.

Innovation is something that human beings were designed to do. We were born to have lightbulb moments. To have a thousand little lightbulbs going off all the time. Those "thousand little lightbulb" moments can start something huge.

I've been passionate about taking steps in a slightly different direction my whole life. Ever since I won a national "Design a Stamp" competition at around age eight, the whole process of creating, making, and experimenting has been in my blood. It's been something I've actively pursued.

A small step is often all it takes to start off down the innovation highway.

For me, though, creating by itself wasn't enough. I've also always had a fascination with behaviour, people and performance. That's what took me into the corporate world sixteen years ago, which was where my new education began.

However, I found my life was balanced best when I had a foot in both the creative and corporate worlds; and when I mixed my creative mind and imagination with my love of connecting with people. I found my true "geek out" spot where creativity, learning, people and passion meet.

Just like anyone else, I've had frustrations and ups and downs in my journey. I've learnt some great things on the way, and made plenty of mistakes. I've pivoted, twisted, turned, leapt, and soared. And importantly, I've had a whole lot of fun and a rich life through embracing my creativity.

That's what I want to share with you. So in this book, I've collected the insights and stories I've gained from mashing up the creative and corporate landscapes. The possibilities are endless when you embrace your creative self and look at the world with different eyes.

This innovation stuff can be a whole lot of fun. Yes, times are different, but that's not a bad thing. It's exciting. And over time, I've found some common principles that can help you kickstart a culture of innovation – one that drives great ideas, services, products, and results.

Let's face it: change is constant (and unless you live under a rock, you've no doubt heard that countless times before). The question is, do you want that change to fill you with discomfort and panic? Or do you want to feel like there's never been a better time to be in business?

If you want the second option, let's get that process started. Let's light your curiosity fire. Let's pull a few levers so you can easily take a few small steps to the left or right. Let's create a few small shifts that will enable you to embrace the new opportunities that exist. It's not hard.

Importantly, let's kickstart a culture that produces a thousand little lightbulb moments in your business and your team.

When I was researching this book, the biggest thing that jumped out for me was the importance of people. Every leader I interviewed said that with great people, anything was possible. I'm writing this book with that in mind.

People are the heart and soul of a culture of innovation. Absolutely, other things need to be in place too; but people are the spark that make innovation happen. People, not processes, drive an innovative culture. And this book will give some great insight into practical ways to not only light the innovation fire within you, but within your people and your organisation too.

Once that fire is alight, it's almost impossible to put out. That's when you have a culture of innovation: a constant stream of lightbulb moments and fresh thinking. A great culture makes great things possible. This, in turn, makes work an enjoyable place to be; and has a huge impact on the rest of your life as well. It's a wonderful space to be in.

I absolutely promise you that great things are possible when you make those small shifts in direction. And before you know it, you'll create the potential for a thousand little lightbulbs to go off all the time.

The facts about what's happening

I mentioned in the last chapter that "business as usual" is *not* the new normal.

The natures of both the global and Australian economies are changing at pace. Even if you fled for the hills with no computer or mobile, and only tins of beans and a survival guide for company, you'd still notice that things were very different.

(Speaking of "different", this is *easily* the driest chapter in the book. I had to deep-dive into a LOT of research to give you a clear sense of how things really are right now, and this chapter is the result. Just stick with me: it's important that you know this stuff, and I promise the pace shifts dramatically after Chapter 2.)

An era of new technologies, such as artificial intelligence, genetics, robotics, machine learning, nanotechnology, 3D printing and biotechnology has already begun. Significant developments have taken place in these fields; and the world is now on the threshold of embracing smart systems, including smart grids, smart farms, and smart cities. In fact, with all this smartness, the term "smarty pants" may no longer be a slur – I'm pretty sure that pants are getting smarter too.

The reality is that the world has already ushered in a fourth industrial revolution, with myriad applications of new-generation technologies.

Due to these changes, workers' skill profiles and job requirements are shifting rapidly. Five years from now, over one-third (35%) of the skills that are considered important in today's workforce will have changed[1]. Jobs that exist now will be gone, replaced by jobs that don't currently exist.

The World Economic Forum lists creativity, which it defines as "the ability to come up with unusual or clever ideas about a given topic or situation" as the third top skill that will be needed for employment in 2020[2]. In 2015, they listed it as the tenth top skill. Perhaps not surprisingly, they list Emotional Intelligence as the sixth needed to thrive in 2020.

PwC recently released their 20th CEO survey[3], which covered 1,379 CEOs from 79 countries. Most CEOs agreed that the hardest skills are those that can't be performed by machines; and that "creativity and innovation" is one of these. It's also pertinent that at least 77% of the CEOs surveyed faced difficulty in recruiting people with creativity and innovation skills.

Things are shifting. Creativity is no longer a "nice to have". It's now essential. In this environment, how will Australia adapt and flourish?

More importantly: what's the current state of innovation in Australia?

Well, let me tell you: Australia has a bit of an innovation problem. Compared to other nations, we rank pretty low.

Let's look at the facts

Forbes has been producing a list of the 100 most innovative companies in the world for the last six years. The latest release from September 2016 doesn't feature a single Australian company[4].

Number of companies	Country
49	USA
8	Japan
7	UK
4	France
2	Denmark
2	Switzerland
1	Germany
Nil	Australia

Meanwhile in 2017, **Bloomberg** published its innovation index report[5], which considered all countries – in both developed and emerging economies. The report focused on seven areas of activities that included:

a)   Research and development
b)   Manufacturing
c)   Productivity
d)   High-tech density
e)   Post-secondary education
f)   Research personnel
g)   Patents activity

Australia didn't rank in the top five for *any* of these fields.

Overall ranking of the top ten innovative countries, which is derived from the average of the above seven measures, is shown below.

Ranks	Country
1	South Korea
2	Sweden
3	Germany
4	Switzerland
5	Finland
6	Singapore
7	Japan
8	Denmark
9	USA
10	Israel

Australia doesn't appear *anywhere* on this list. (In fact, we come in at 18th.)

(OK, let's stop and breathe for a moment. If you're getting a little bored, or going a little crazy, stick with me. I know there are a *lot* of stats here, but they're moving you towards an important point. And if you're not clear on that point, the rest of the book might not make as much sense to you.)

Cornell University, INSEAD and the **World Intellectual Property Organization (WIPO)** jointly publish the Global Innovation Index (GII) for the countries of the world. The core of the GII Report consists of a ranking of world economies' innovation capabilities and results.

According to the GII 2017, Australia ranks outside the top 20 for Innovation Status[6].

Rank	Country	Score
1	Switzerland	67.99
2	Sweden	63.82
3	Netherlands	63.36
4	USA	61.40
5	United Kingdom	60.89
6	Denmark	58.70
7	Singapore	58.69
8	Finland	58.49
9	Germany	58.39
10	Ireland	58.13
11	South Korea	57.71
12	Luxembourg	56.40
13	Iceland	55.76
14	Japan	54.72
15	France	54.18
16	Hong Kong	53.88
17	Israel	53.88
18	Canada	53.65
19	Norway	53.14
20	Austria	53.10
23	Australia	51.83

(Mmmm, this is all still pretty dry isn't it? But seriously: don't skip to the next chapter. We're on the downhill run through these facts now. I have faith in your ability to take them in. You can do it!)

Then, there's the **2016 Australian Innovation System Report (AISR)**. According to this report:

~ Less than 1% of all Australian business were classed as "innovation-active", spending at least $5 million on innovation[7].

~ In the list of all 33 OECD countries, Australia also ranks incredibly low on innovation in organisational or marketing methods, at 30th position for large businesses, and 31st for SMEs, (Small to Medium Enterprises, classed as 10–249 employees)[8].

~ We rank 28th for the manufacturing sector, and 29th for the services sector among all OECD countries[9].

~ In product or process innovations, Australia ranks *last* in a group of 28 OECD countries[10].

~ Australian businesses' Research and Development spending has been declining since the 2008 economic crisis. We currently rank 14th out of 36 OECD countries in R&D spending[11].

~ New-to-market innovation (new to industry, new to world, and new to Australia) has also been declining since the 2008 economic crisis.

~ As far as Innovation Novelty (creating new products that have never existed before) goes, Australia is a follower, not an innovation leader. Only 5.5% of surveyed businesses created completely new-to-market goods and services[12].

~ According to the AISR 2014 report, nearly half (44.8 %) of the businesses surveyed had nobody assigned exclusively to innovation. Respondents to the survey often had no idea how much their firm spent on innovation efforts[13].

According to a **2013 report by the Institute of Chartered Accountants Australia**:

~ A significantly lower proportion of businesses here in Australia innovate (53%) compared to any other country in the EU.

For example, our rate is far lower than an economic powerhouse like Germany, where 80% of businesses reported innovation activity[14].

~ Additionally, innovation rarely features in the business performance measurement systems of Australian firms. If something isn't measured, there's a very high probability that it's seen as unimportant[15].

~ On an environmental level, Australia faces significant threats. Pollution, biodiversity losses, and climate change will all significantly affect our lifestyle, natural ecosystems, and health.

Yet, in an area where innovation is mission-critical, Australia ranks poorly on Business Environmental Performance when compared with other developed countries of the world. Only 10% of Australian businesses can reduce their environmental impact in relation to water, energy, and air pollution[16].

So what? Are we really backward?

Not at all. Those average results are surprising for a few reasons:

1. Australian CEOs rate innovation very highly.

2. Innovation makes a big difference to the bottom dollar of Australian businesses.

3. Australia has a very talented workforce.

So we should be great at innovation! Here are the facts...

Australian CEOs actually rate innovation very highly:

~ In 2016, **KPMG** released a Global CEO outlook study that encompassed 1,300 global CEOs, of whom 53 were from Australian firms. It's clear that innovation is on everyone's radar: a large proportion of those CEOs (79%) had embraced either strategic, accelerated, or foundational innovation approaches as a key corporate strategy[17]. And 77% of global CEOs had also included clear objectives for innovation in their business strategy[18].

HOW

will *your* organisation thrive as the world around you rapidly changes?

~ "Fostering innovation" also emerged as one of the top three strategic priorities among 28% of Australian CEOs. In contrast, only 21% of global CEOs emphasised "fostering innovation" as a strategy. Moreover, 45% of the Australian CEOs pursued an "accelerated approach to innovation", compared to 35% of CEOs globally.

It's interesting to see that 28% of Australian CEOs embraced disruptive technology for innovation, which is significantly higher than their counterparts (18%) globally.

Innovation makes a big difference to the bottom line of Australian businesses:

~ Every $1 invested in innovation activities returns $2 in revenue. Accordingly, investing $30 billion in innovation returns $60 billion in revenue[19].

~ Compared with non-innovation-active businesses, those who are innovation-active in Australia are responsible for generating[20]:

- 1.4x higher income from sales of goods and services

- 2x higher productivity

- 1.4x higher profitability

- 3x higher employment

- 5x higher exports of goods

So there's a *really* good business case for embracing innovation and being prepared to doing things differently.

Australia has a very talented workforce:

The **Global Creativity Index (GCI)** is a broad-based measure for advanced economic growth and sustainable prosperity that's based on the three Ts of economic development: talent, technology, and tolerance. The GCI rates and ranks 139 nations worldwide on each of these dimensions, and on our overall measures of creativity and prosperity.

According to the GCI, Australia has the most talented workforce – we're ahead of the US, New Zealand, Canada, and Nordic countries[21]. This is measured in two ways:

~ **By the share of the workforce classed as "creative"** – workers in science, technology, and engineering; arts, culture, entertainment, and the media; business and management; and education, healthcare, and law.

~ **By the share of adults with higher education.**

In short, there is brilliant potential in Australia; and there's a great possibility to become more competitive and productive IF the country as a whole taps into its creativity and ability to innovate.

In areas such as process innovation, the Australian mining sector is around twice as innovative as their US counterparts. And many of Australia's service sector firms are more innovative than their counterparts in the US too[22].

(You're probably now thinking, "Holy shit, are we almost there?" The good news is that the answer is yes. Just a little bit more…)

So, what's the problem?

Australia seems to have the right ingredients for innovation. In my research for this book, every senior leader or partner I interviewed said that they rated innovation as important to their future, giving it an average importance score of 8–9 out of 10. However, they ranked their current innovation performance as closer to 3–4 out of 10.

The reasons they gave for this were:

~ **Not sure where to start:** the pace of market disruption is so great that they knew they'd be left behind unless they embraced innovation. However, they're busy doing other things, and feel stumped at how to kick off innovation and are lagging behind.

~ **No time for innovation:** they saw innovation as just another "to do" on an already-crowded list. Additionally, they didn't measure innovation in their KPIs and it wasn't rewarded, so their people didn't give it any time.

~ **Not having the right people:** leaders knew that people with great talent could literally smash whatever the market threw at them, yet they struggled to get the best people and hang onto them.

Despite its relative age, a 2007 McKinsey survey on innovation inhibitors is still spot on today[23]:

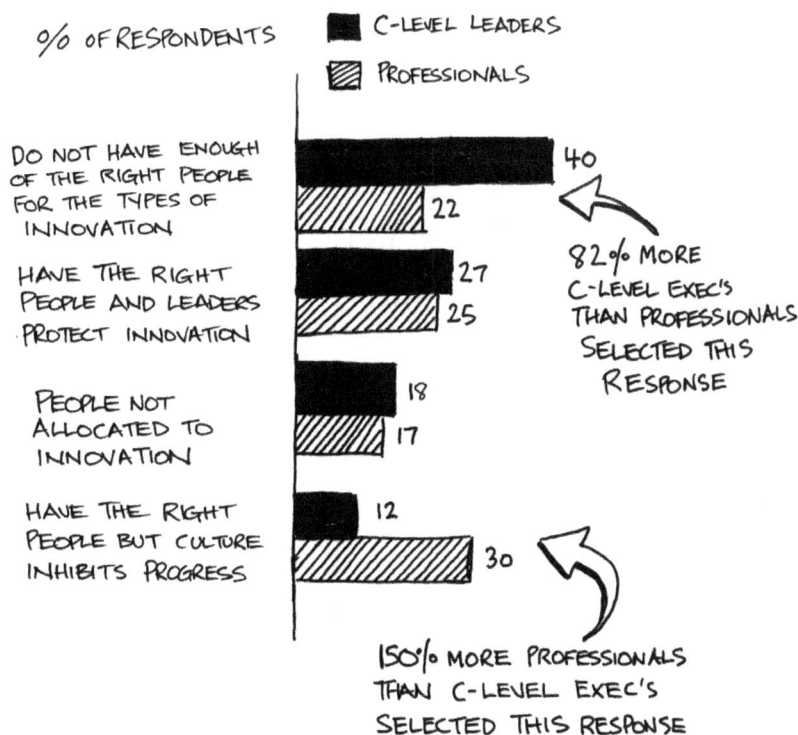

% OF RESPONDENTS

■ C-LEVEL LEADERS
▨ PROFESSIONALS

DO NOT HAVE ENOUGH OF THE RIGHT PEOPLE FOR THE TYPES OF INNOVATION — 40 / 22

82% MORE C-LEVEL EXEC'S THAN PROFESSIONALS SELECTED THIS RESPONSE

HAVE THE RIGHT PEOPLE AND LEADERS PROTECT INNOVATION — 27 / 25

PEOPLE NOT ALLOCATED TO INNOVATION — 18 / 17

HAVE THE RIGHT PEOPLE BUT CULTURE INHIBITS PROGRESS — 12 / 30

150% MORE PROFESSIONALS THAN C-LEVEL EXEC'S SELECTED THIS RESPONSE

In other words, innovation revolves around empowering great people, and having those great people create a great culture.

How will YOUR organisation thrive as the world around you rapidly changes?

Will you get the right people on board, and empower them to innovate and create?

If you feel yourself starting to panic again, relax: there IS some good news

1. **Creating a culture of innovation starts with small steps.** This book will provide concrete steps to shift the way that your people think, behave, and collaborate; and make it fun in the process.

2. **An innovation mindset doesn't take more time**, it just takes a shift in perspective. Great ideas are everywhere if we only open our eyes.

3. **Your organisation already has great people.** They just aren't using their full creative potential to drive innovation. You need to learn how to tap that creative potential.

Your organisation's culture of innovation will be driven by you and your people, once you unlock your creative potential – and theirs – and let it thrive. You're sitting on a rocket ship that's waiting to take off. (Having said that, sitting *on* the rocket may be slightly painful – so perhaps move inside it and strap in!)

Re-light the creativity your team was born with, and build a culture of innovation that creates an ever-flowing stream of brilliant ideas, market-leading thinking, products and results.

INNOVATION happens When CREATIVITY, LEARNING, PEOPLE  & Passion Combine

We've been innovating since Day 1

Look around you.
Look at what's on your desk.
When you step outside at lunchtime, look up.
Look wide, and look all around.

Everything you see (other than nature) has come to exist through human creativity and innovation. Someone made a choice to create something. They decided to combine certain elements to create something new.

Innovation, however, is nothing new.

When you think about it, innovation has been happening for a long, long time. It's in our blood. Take your mind back... way, way back to prehistoric times, when humanity was much younger.

When prehistoric Sue was building a shelter, and decided to create a roof by weaving extra-large leaves instead of twigs to keep the kids dry, that was innovation.

YOUR
brain is designed
to be an imagination
station.

When caveman Theodore decided to design a spear instead of a rock to throw at the mammoth, innovation (and a speedier dinner) happened.

When Beryl got curious about what would happen if she controlled the heat of the spreading wildfire instead of running from it, she had an innovation mindset.

From the moment Barry suggested to Colin that they round the edges of the square stones they were using as wheels, innovation was unstoppable.

Taming animals, farming, forming trade... the list goes on. This innovation stuff is nothing new at all. It's the most logical and normal thing we do.

It's natural progress.

Almost everything we love and enjoy has come from innovation. It's all been created. We live great lives today because of innovation. Huge problems get solved, and will continue to be solved, every day through innovation.

Imagine if Sue had just stayed under her leaky shelter, grumbling away and ignoring the extra-large, weavable leaves she could see. Her kids would have stayed damp and miserable, and been dripped on every time it rained.

Ditto if Theodore had decided that throwing small rocks at the mammoth as it ran through the village was the only way to go. The village would have stayed hungry (and possibly squashed). Luckily, Theodore was curious, so he explored other ideas.

What if Beryl had never asked herself, "I wonder…" when she saw the wildfire? Spoiler alert: we'd never have tasted a cooked dinner, and we'd still be freezing in winter.

What if Barry and Colin had sat back and said that inventing the wheel was someone else's job? Or if Colin had said that change was unnatural, and that they'd been pushing things around on square wheels for a long time?

Can you imagine how bumpy a car ride would be?

So let's be very clear:

~ Being curious about things is normal.

~ Having an imagination is normal.

~ Being creative is normal.

~ Innovating is normal.

There's nothing new in this process.

What's changed over time is people's view on this process – especially in the corporate landscape. For many people, the view has shifted significantly.

Innovation has become something that other people do. It's for people who wear jeans and t-shirts to work. It's for people who:

~ Eat quinoa and kale salads

~ Drink craft beer

~ Listen to music in super-sized headphones

~ Run startups from their garage

It's become something that very talented people think they can't do. They've started to believe that imagination is something for other people.

Harry Potter author JK Rowling said, "Imagination is not only the uniquely human capacity to envision that which is not, and, therefore, the foundation of all invention and innovation. In its arguably most transformative and revelatory capacity, it is the power that enables us to empathise with humans whose experiences we have never shared."

Your brain is designed to be an imagination station. So, let's tap back into that curious, creative spirit that your ancestors had.

Let's tap back into what should be completely normal. Let's get curious once again.

Let's create a thousand little lightbulb moments. Exciting times are ahead.

Reframing the innovation challenge

Let's not shy away from the fact that innovation can be bit of a buzz-word – one that people want to avoid, especially if it's been bandied about as the "Next Big Thing".

But it doesn't have to be that way. Let's see how you can make innovation into something interesting and fun for your team.

My first job in the corporate space was in Corporate Training. I remember the first time my director asked me if I could teach creativity. Despite my creative background and visual arts degree, I was stumped. I connected with a bunch of creative friends and asked what was possible.

They pointed me in the direction of a few different theories. As an artist, I was truthfully confused by this academic approach. It was a completely different mindset to what I'd experienced myself. I had plenty of creativity, and so did my friends. But how do you teach creativity as a set skill?

A few months later, another director asked if I could do anything with my art background for a client offsite. Again, this was a totally new paradigm, but I was up for the challenge.

So I reverse-engineered the creative process I used for painting, and created an experience that, bit by bit, built the team's confidence. All the while, I was teaching the necessary skills so that each person could create something that looked awesome.

The feedback was great. (In fact, it wasn't just great: it was outstanding.)

People entered the room thinking that they weren't creative; then left thinking they were. It was a complete shift for everyone.

And it made me realise that creativity *wasn't* a standalone thinking skill.

Instead, it was a combination of thinking, action, learning and confidence, with some passion thrown in. That was a reframe for me (and the participants).

We live the stories we tell ourselves: they manifest in our behaviour and our actions. If we constantly tell ourselves that we aren't good at something, we won't be. And what we think then drives what we do.

What do you tell *yourself* about innovation?

~ If you tell yourself that innovation is something that everyone else looks after, that will be the case.

~ If you keep saying that innovation is just too much to take on, it will be.

~ If you keep saying that you don't have a creative bone in your body, that will be the case too.

YOUR
innovation strategy must include these three words: *people, people* and *people.*

~ If your directors keep thinking that they're too important for this creative fluff, they will be (and the "creative fluff" won't happen).

~ If you tell yourself you can't share your ideas because they're not perfect, then you won't share anything, and innovation won't occur.

It's time to start thinking differently about innovation, and reframe it.

Your innovation reframe could take many forms. It could be around:

~ A thriving company

~ Doing the absolute best that you can

~ Making a massive impact

~ Leaving a legacy that drives success

~ Taking your team to a better place after they've worked with you

Regardless, the challenge of innovation is about fulfilling your potential.

It's about enjoying every day. It's about feeling good inside. It's about being a thought leader who constantly supplies fresh thinking. And it's about driving an organisation that makes a huge impact and solves wicked problems.

If the idea of innovation seems daunting, try reframing it and replacing the word *innovation* with *fresh thinking*.

I've had plenty of conversations where people aren't sure about all this innovation stuff. I haven't yet, however, talked to anyone who isn't interested in fresh thinking.

Fresh thinking provides more options and more chances of getting a great result. It allows organisations to be disruptors, rather than disrupted. A fresh thinker is someone who always sees Options #1–#10, rather than just Options #1 and #2. Fresh thinkers are people who drive a team that's dynamic, responsive and energetic in its thinking, rather than one with stable but very predictable and linear thinking.

The reframe you need is that innovation does not belong in the "too-hard basket". It belongs in the everyday, absolutely-normal basket. It's not something that Marketing should take care of. It's not something for organic hipsters on a hand-crafted unicycle delivering wholemeal cupcakes. It's something that everyone needs to be involved in.

It's about naturally getting the best from your potential.

Try this switch:

> *Mindset 1: I must be innovative. Quick, do something! Oh shit, that didn't work. Let's stop. Too hard!*

Reframe it:

> *Mindset 2: I want to develop a culture in our company where market-leading thinking drives great ideas, products, services, and results.*

Mindset 2 is an innovation mindset; and it should be your normal mindset. It should be what your company continuously does to make a difference – to thrive, to have great people, and to make a serious impact.

It's also time to think a little differently about the challenge of innovation, and reframe some of your thought patterns.

Tony Robbins speaks of having a more transformational vocabulary. He says, "The words that we attach to our experience become our experience, regardless of whether it's objectively accurate or not. Therefore, if we want to change our lives and our destiny, we need to consciously choose the words we use to describe our emotional states."

So it's time to change your vocabulary and language around innovation. Change it from being "hard work" to just being "normal"; and from "stressful" to "enjoyable".

It's time to embrace what you were born to do, and watch the good times roll.

Innovation is a *people* thing

Finally, it's time to reframe the role of *people* in innovation.

As Walt Disney said, "You can dream, create, design, and build the most beautiful place in the world, but it requires people to make it a reality."

Let's be VERY clear: innovation is ALL about people.

People drive innovation. Innovation doesn't happen to people: instead, people create innovation.

Innovation *will not* happen in your company without great people – people whose innovation fire has been lit. People are the starting point for all innovation. It's not systems, processes or things – it's people.

This is where many large companies can get it wrong. They focus on things rather than people. Things can't drive a culture of innovation.

The recently appointed Chancellor of The University of Technology Sydney (UTS) Catherine Livingstone echoes similar sentiments from a position of strength. As a former CSIRO Chair, President of the Business Council of Australia, Fellow of the Australian Academy of Science, and CEO and Managing Director of Cochlear, she has both brilliant real-world experience and insight.

In her first speech as UTS Chancellor, Livingstone spoke about people driving innovation, and then everything else happening around that. She said, "The starting point for any discussion on innovation has to be people. Not governments, not institutions, not businesses, but the people inside them. It's an intensely human activity – minds rubbing on minds."

Then, in an interview with ABC Radio, she said that one problem with innovation is that the community thinks it's something done to them, not by them. Innovation is a very human process, not a government initiative.

The importance of people is nothing new.

When I was doing research with senior leaders and partners for this book, one of the consistent themes was their absolute need for great people. Not for systems or remuneration or structure, but for people.

No matter what sector or type of company the leaders came from, they listed quality people as key. I constantly heard, "Simon, if we can get and keep the right people, we can achieve anything. Market disruption doesn't matter when you have great people."

Your innovation strategy must include these three words: people, people and people.

Machines don't come up with vitality and fresh thinking. Nor do systems. Only people do that.

Great people already exist in your company. Everyone on your team and within your organisation has a set of unbelievably creative skills. It's just that they've either forgotten how to use them, or had them shut down so many times that they don't bother using them any more. That, or they make the conscious decision to leave those creative skills at home.

Incidentally, "being shut down" can be caused by their Ogre (the monster voice inside all of us that criticises every attempt at creativity we make – more on this later) or by other people. Either way, what a waste.

Your people have a fire inside them – it just needs to be rekindled. Like all fires, theirs will start off small at first… but it can take off and spread. The great news with a creativity and innovation fire is that once you've lit it, it's easy to keep alight. (The other great news is that the book you're holding will show you how to do this, without requiring you to become a bearded hipster or eat your weight in kale.)

Imagination and creativity are what make us unique as humans. They're fun, free, and they feel good. Why wouldn't you want something like this in your life? Once the fire is lit, you can keep fanning the slow-burning embers whenever you need them, and you're away.

The answer to every company's future lies in the heart and soul of its people – in tapping into their innovation potential. George Lois, the legendary ad man and creator, said, "Creativity can solve almost any problem – the creative act, the defeat of habit by originality, overcomes everything."

Remember: no one has a monopoly on kick-arse ideas

Great ideas aren't just the domain of the leadership group, the creative department, HR or the marketing team. In fact, great ideas and market-leading thinking should come from everywhere in your company – because they exist everywhere.

They exist in every employee that you have. The problem is that those ideas are often ignored. When was the last time you really listened to absolutely everyone in your company? When was the last time you really threw the "ideas net" far and wide?

We all have great ideas. Everyone in your company has their own unique set of circumstances, life experiences, and ways of looking at the world. As such, the way they connect a given set of dots is different. Breakthroughs happen when people connect the same dots in different ways. For example:

~ Apple connected the worlds of design and technology, or as Steve Jobs called them, *technology* and *liberal arts*.

~ Airbnb initially connected the world of spare bedrooms and people's need for accommodation.

~ Spotify connected people's love of music with internet connectivity (and the guilt of illegally downloading music).

~ Australia's Divvy Parking connected drivers' frustrations at the expense and scarcity of inner city parking with owners and businesses who had spare, unused parking spots.

People in your company who have absolutely nothing to do with your role or the problems you want to solve will bring a fresh set of eyes to your situation. They'll connect the dots in different ways. They'll walk around the problem looking in, rather than being up to their necks in it (which is where you are). So…

~ The delivery people in your company will each have a unique perspective.

~ Your EA will have yet another frame of reference.

~ The people in Purchasing will see things differently to you.

All the people in your company will have great perspectives and experiences. These people will have great ideas, and they need to be heard.

This is why I struggle a little with the words "creative department". I don't have a problem with the people working in the department – not at all. But wouldn't a better framework be "creative company" or "company full of creative departments"? Obviously, not everyone will design brochures or campaigns, but everyone should feel confident about offering their fresh insights.

The problem with having a "creative department" is that it can mean everyone else leaves coming up with ideas to that department. It also sends the subliminal message: "Don't share your ideas. We don't need them. After all, we have a creative department for that."

One of Google's Innovation Pillars is "Look for ideas everywhere". Susan Wojcicki, Google's former Senior Vice President of Advertising and current YouTube CEO, said, "As the leader of our ads products, I want to hear ideas from everyone – and that includes our partners, advertisers, and all of the people on my team. I also want to be a part of the conversations Googlers are having in the hallways."

It doesn't matter where you work, or what your role is within a company. No matter how far removed from the problem someone seems, there are great ideas everywhere. So get out and hear them. Connect with others, and seek their valuable perspective and input.

Remember: innovation starts with people. Not with systems or things, but with *people*.

There are already great people in your organisation, and there could already be a thousand little lightbulbs going off all over your company.

Make sure you see and hear them all.

Brain basics 101

Your brain is pretty smart. It's amazing. If your brain were a person, it would be in both the super-hip and the super-smart crowd.

Your brain's got it going on. It's clever, and it knows it as well.

How does your brain operate?

There's so much stuff going on in the world; so your brain labels things and experiences, then stores the information to use in similar situations in future. In other words, your brain works very hard to make life easier for you. (Thanks, brain. That's really helpful.)

As an example, when you were young, you might have reached out to pick a rose. It looked so bright and nice… but then OWWWW! What happened? The spikes hurt, and you cried.

Once your tears dried, your brain stored that connection, labelling it "pain/flowers" or something similar. And then next time you saw a rose, you knew there'd be spikes, so you just looked and smiled. (Thanks again, brain. Very helpful.)

That process has continued on throughout your life. Things happen, your brain labels them, stores information about them, and uses it again in future. That's great, because it makes your life much easier. You do things more efficiently, and waste less time. Absolutely brilliant. (No really. Thanks, brain. You're totally awesome.)

Because let's face it. When you're rushing off to work in the morning, you don't want to brainstorm what you need to do. You just want to get up, get into the zone, and open the "Getting ready for work" file.

Ask yourself: which scenario below works better?

Scenario 1: *Alarm beep, beep, beep: shower, grab clothes, drink, toast, sprint for train – all is good.*

Scenario 2: *Alarm, beep, beep, beep: arghhhh, what happens next? Let's look at the options. I could lay here a while, I could do some research on my phone, I could listen to the alarm ringtone for ages, I could have a shower. Mmmm, shower seems the best option. OK, shower's done. What should I wear to work? There are so many options. I have this great velour tracksuit that Uncle Alex bought back from Hawaii. These great trousers could go with any number of these t-shirts. Hang on, it's going to be hot. Will my swimsuit work for my meeting? Let's try. (10 mins later) OK, the business suit works. All right, let's think about breakfast. What happens if I crack an egg on my cornflakes?*

I could go on, but you get it. You have a great collection of labels, files, cupboards and storage systems in your brain. Your brain always works for you. Or does it?

Imagine this.

Scenario 1: *You get to work. Sarah comes into your office and says, "I have a great idea."*

Your brain kicks into action. It already has a label for Sarah. You've been here before, and she always has ideas that take up your time. You say, "I'm under the pump here, Sarah. Can you come back and see me next week?"

Sarah leaves, crestfallen; then resigns and launches her own startup. Word spreads, and six of your best team members jump ship with her. Opportunity missed. (Thanks, brain. What type of label was that?)

Scenario 2: Someone calls you on the way home to invite you kayaking on Saturday morning. Your brain rummages around the group of labels and files in your head. It comes back with, "OK, you tried this 20 years ago, fell in the water and got cold. Don't do that again."

You tell your friend, "No thanks, I'm fine."

Then, on Sunday, you bump into a group of your friends. Everyone's buzzing about their beautiful experience kayaking on the water. Calm river, sunny weather, instructor with the group, and great coffee at the end. They can't wait to do it next time. Opportunity missed again. (Thanks, brain. What type of label was THAT?)

As you can see, your brain can be both a best friend and a hindrance. (Thanks, brain.)

How can you harness the wonders of your brain?

Don't worry: your brain's labelling system is great. You do, however, need to recognise that the classification system doesn't work for every situation. Your experiences, and the labels and files you create for them, give you a certain way of looking at the world. They create a set of blinkers (like the ones a horse wears) for you.

Those blinkers then have a big impact on the way that you look at the world. It wasn't long ago that we had no labels in our brains for Facebook or Twitter. There wasn't a file for cloud-based software, or crowd funding, or Netflix and video streaming. There wasn't a label for smart phones or 3D printing. (And yes, some leaders with tight blinkers may still not have a file in their brain for these things. Imagine how much good that's doing them.)

In a more disruptive environment, where innovation and fresh thinking are essential, the challenge is recognising your current filing system may not have enough labels to adapt and thrive. So you need to take off your blinkers, and invite your brain to open and create new files.

That doesn't mean that your life experiences and the files your brain has created are useless. Not at all. Each time you generate a new file, it creates new patterns and networks with your old files. That, in turn, creates a new way of thinking and looking at the world.

But not everyone is comfortable with that way of looking at the world. Too many people struggle to shift from their "Business as Usual" style of thinking, because they're too used to thinking and operating in certain way.

The problem is that in doing so, they limit their brain's potential.

Imagine this

Two people walk into a job interview for a very important role in your team. You know the battle for the right people is a hard one, and you're desperate to get the right fit for your team.

***Person 1, Agatha**, comes in and says, "I promise to use half my brain here."*

***Person 2, Ethel**, says, "I promise to use all of my brain here."*

It's a pretty easy choice, right? You don't say to Agatha, "Great, just the type of half-brained worker I've been looking for! Come on in. Join the team. You'll be a leader in this organisation soon."

The problem is that Agatha exists everywhere. She's everyone who goes through life without acknowledging the great potential of the other half their brain.

It's not deliberate. It's just that bad habits take over.

Let's do a little bit of brain basics 101

Your brain is a pretty intricate and complicated organ. If it were a person, you'd invite it to every dinner party... but you probably wouldn't want to be cornered with it after one too many reds.

"Wow," you might find yourself saying. "That brain is a deep and complex person. Interesting, sophisticated... yet so perplexing."

With that in mind, I want to keep this section as simple as possible.

Let's start by acknowledging that the brain is an amazingly complex thing, and that different parts of it control different things...

Now. If this book were only about brains, I could get super technical at this point. Instead, here's what you need to know for your innovation and creativity drive.

Your brain is divided into two hemispheres. Each hemisphere controls the opposite side of your body, and they're linked in the middle by fibres that deliver messages from one side to the other.

IF

your brain were
a person, it would
be in both the
super-hip and the
super-smart crowd.

Many people also believe that each hemisphere exclusively controls different thinking and emotional functions. And while that idea has been scientifically debunked, it's still a good metaphor that can help you to understand the creative process. So bearing that disclaimer in mind, think of:

~ **Your left hemisphere** as controlling language, logic, maths, analysis and anything serious.

~ **Your right hemisphere** as being fluid, flowing, creative, musical and humorous.

In this model, these two sides are designed to work in perfect harmony with each other, and as counterbalances and best friends to each other's greatness. So within this metaphor:

~ The left side provides the detail, while the right side sees the big picture.

~ The left side hears the "I'm OK" response, but the right side sees the speaker's face is really sad, and prompts you to dig deeper.

~ The left side wants to get somewhere as quickly as possible so you'll be on time, while the right side wants to stop and soak up the atmosphere and sights along the way.

The idea of the two sides working in harmony was strongly highlighted for me when I worked in England, back before I had children.

I had a foot in both the corporate and the creative spaces; and it was perfect for me.

One job was as an account manager, where I'd also facilitate conferences and workshops for my training organisation. I came to an arrangement with my director where I could work part-time in this role; and that's when things really kicked off for me.

My other job was lecturing at the National Gallery of England about their amazing collection of paintings. Equalled only by the Louvre in Paris, the Gallery has the best collection of Western art in the world. This was an amazing job. I worked with visiting groups to bring the awe-inspiring artworks to life for them. Essentially, I opened their eyes to what they were looking at, and got them excited about what they saw.

Neither job would have been perfect on its own. But together, they created my happy place. They provided a perfect blend of the creative mixed with the strategic. Of structure mixed with free flow. The different styles of thinking and operating that these roles required really helped each individual part of my professional life to thrive.

How does just using one type of thinking play out?

The problem is that for many people, one type of thinking (or one side of the brain, in our metaphor) gets all the attention. It "works out" much more than the other one. And, just like any imbalance, this causes problems.

Although your brain is an organ, it has all the metaphorical characteristics of a muscle. Yes, this chapter is full of metaphors; and although it may sound weird to call your brain a muscle, it responds exactly the same way that muscles do. The more you use your brain, the stronger it gets. It doesn't develop new mass the way a muscle would, but it does develop its ability to make new connections and create new files.

Dr. Michael Merzenich, PhD and author of *Soft-Wired: How the New Science of Brain Plasticity Can Change Your Life*, says that our brains are "plastic" (i.e. constantly developing) if we treat them the right way. If you exercise your brain properly, it will continue to develop. If you ignore it and let it sit idle, it will deteriorate and atrophy.

If you don't exercise the part of your brain that does a particular kind of thinking, it gets weaker and weaker. And most people just don't exercise their whole brain equally.

Imagine working out your body the way you work out your brain

Think of it like this... imagine winter has just finished. After three months of comfort food and red wine, like many of us, you're carrying a little extra body baggage. Of course, during the cold months, that's not an issue. You're all rugged up, so your awesome body is hidden under thick clothes.

Now, though, you know summer is on its way. This jolts you into action and gets you busy. You join the thousands of others hitting boot camp every spring, and get into it. You exercise, lift weights, eat a great diet, and basically spend four weeks working hard and sweating.

Then that first hot day hits, and everything feels tight and trim again. Your summer mojo is back! You hit the beach, dish out a few pleasant nods as you dash through the crowds, and celebrate inside as you dive into the waves.

The next day, though, when you're back at the gym, you decide to only work out the left side of your body. You've had enough of all that hard work now, and you want to take it easier.

After a while, your left side gets much bigger... but your right side starts looking a little flabby and limp. You don't care though. If you see anyone on the beach, you can just turn your right side away from them. This is great: half the work.

The issues, of course, start to come later. Your best friend asks you to help them lift something heavy. You try, but you can't help: you don't have any strength on your right side. You ask, "Is there anything small that I could lift with just my left hand?"

And the problems with a weak side of your body continue from there:

- *You can't mow the lawns in a straight line.*

- *You can no longer pick up your children, unless it's under one arm.*

- *Your juggling hobby is ruined.*

In my experience, too many people keep exercising their "left-brain" thinking and neglecting their "right". Over time, their left becomes more and more dominant, and the labels and files they create have that "left-brain" focus. They only look at the world in a "left-brain way".

They usually don't notice they're doing this, because they're only connecting with other people who share a similar view. All the while, their "right-brain" thinking becomes weaker and weaker. They do a degree that discourages whole-brain thinking, and then they work for an organisation that only rewards "left brain"-behaviour.

This "left-dominated" mindset would be fine if the world would just stay the same, and if the market weren't being constantly disrupted. But that's not the case.

Remember Sarah? The woman who left and took half of your best and brightest to be on her team? Well, she's now on the front cover of Forbes Magazine's "Hot 30 under 30" issue. She's heading up a 400-person company, and solving the world's greatest problems. She always went on about this innovation stuff. Sarah was some-one who used both types of thinking.

Actor and comedian John Cleese has great insight on this.

He says, "We all operate in two contrasting modes, which might be called open and closed. The open mode is more relaxed, more receptive, more exploratory, more democratic, more playful and more humorous. The closed mode is the tighter, more rigid, more hierarchical, more tunnel-visioned. Most people, unfortunately spend most of their time in the closed mode. Not that the closed mode cannot be helpful. If you are leaping a ravine, the moment of takeoff is a bad time for considering alternative strategies.

When you charge the enemy machine-gun post, don't waste energy trying to see the funny side of it. Do it in the "closed" mode. But the moment the action is over, try to return to the "open" mode – to open your mind again to all the feedback from your action that enables you to tell whether the action has been successful, or whether further action is needed to improve on what you have done. In other words, we must return to the open mode, because in that mode we are the most aware, most receptive, most creative, and therefore at our most intelligent."

We're designed to use both hemispheres of our brains, and we're designed to work with both kinds of thinking. Let me be clear: it's not about one or the other. Left and right are meant to be best friends. They're great counterbalances to each other. They're not meant to work in silos.

There's a place where the free-flow, possibility-rich, emotion-filled, human-centred thinking of the "right" meshes with the logical, analytical and strategic thinking of the "left". That place, where these two styles of thinking and behaviour exist, is innovation. This is what I call the Innovation Sweet Spot.

I once used the Innovation Sweet Spot explanation at an investment bank where I was running a workshop. When I explained that innovation uses all of your brain, I saw the lights go on in the audience. I could feel their palpable sense of relief that innovation wasn't about giving up the things they were already good at. Instead, it's about combining those fantastic skills with new insight and freshness, and reigniting their whole-brain thinking.

Again, it's not about one style of thinking vs. the other. You can have the craziest, wildest ideas in the world – but those ideas still need a real-world blowtorch applied to them. It's about recognising the need for both types of thinking; and knowing when to use (and importantly, when not to use) each one. It's about knowing whether now is the right time for open or closed thinking.

Over time, having both "sides" of the brain ready to go and work with each other just becomes natural. Getting there takes awareness and practice, but this is how our brains are designed to work.

This is a culture of innovation. The culture of a thousand little lightbulbs.

INNOVATION

SWEET SPOT

Even cavemen were creative

I know you don't believe it… but everyone is born creative.

Here's something I've noticed. I love to travel, and one of the things I've picked up is that every indigenous culture does a few things that are almost identical.

They tell stories. They tell their stories through pictures, dancing, music and song. That means they're all creative, and they all do creative things.

We humans were designed to express ourselves creatively. Art, singing, dancing and forming abstract concepts into stories is just part of who we are. It's what enables us to be human. It's part of our DNA, and it's in our soul.

Our brains are designed to make creativity happen.

We've been creatively communicating and expressing our identities for thousands of years. We've done this in a way that engaged all of our senses, to make our stories easy to remember and share with the next generation. Most importantly, each subsequent generation has embraced this aspect of communication, creativity and self-expression. It was just *normal*.

So, what happened?

How did we get to the stage where so many people have no singing, dancing, drawing, painting or other creativity in their lives? Most of us only sing now spontaneously after one too many drinks following the netball grand final. Dancing follows a similar path – only happening after a few too many drinks get our limbs moving at a friend's wedding. As for painting? Go to hell: *that's* not happening, no matter how many drinks we consume.

Caveman story time

Imagine a modern-day, corporate version of caveman story night.

The fire is lit. The kids are sitting close to it. Mum's at the back, sewing animal skins together. Uncle Barry's on one side, sharpening his axe.

Stuart, the chief storyteller, stands up and says, "This evening, our story night will be a little different. I'd like to use this new storytelling tool called PowerPoint. Everyone ready? OK, let's get started.

OK, has anyone seen my clicker? It doesn't seem to be working. Maybe if I point it like this? There, I think I've got it. Now, you won't be able to see the graph on my first slide, but if you could, you'd see that our baby mammoth yield dropped significantly this year."

At this point, the kids start crying, and Uncle Barry drops the axe on his foot as an excuse to leave. Meanwhile, Mum accidentally-on-purpose sews the animal skin to her leg just to relieve the boredom.

You get the picture. Cavemen inherently embraced their creativity. Our modern "Death by PowerPoint" style of communication and expression wouldn't have worked then, and it's no better now.

So why do we use that style? What happened to our creativity?

Picasso said, "Every child is an artist. The problem is how to remain an artist when he grows up".

Kids have this whole innovation stuff sussed. They *rock* innovation. And we can learn great lessons from their approach and mindset.

For example, our family has an endless supply of large cardboard boxes coming into the house. I'm always keen to get rid of them as quickly as possible: to me, they're just another thing to put your foot through in the middle of the night. My children, however, have a different mindset. Where I see mess and clutter, they see possibility and the chance to create.

And create they do.

They create castles, spaceships, cars, cubbies for toys, racing car tracks, cots, tree houses and defence shields. You name it, they see it – and then they create it. The excitement they get from a cardboard box is almost unbelievable.

Sometimes my wife and I are literally scared by the frenzy (and the mess) that we know is coming. Out come the pens, scissors, tape and paper; and away they go.

It's a complete free-for-all.

Young kids are hardwired with a very different *what's possible* framework to adults. They look at the world with a unique and fresh set of eyes. Where we see problems, they see opportunities. Where I see clutter, they see castles. Nothing is off limits.

We all started this way, with a *what's possible* mindset. An *opportunity* mindset. We had creative passion and drive. We could see things that weren't there, and we went and created them. We could look outside of the box (get it? get it?) and not see just cardboard.

This is a wonderful skill, and we were all born with it. I mean, have you ever heard this conversation at a barbecue?

> *"What's the matter with old Dave over there?"*

> *"Oh, didn't you know? He was born uncreative.
>   Poor thing."*

Of course you haven't. It just doesn't happen. We're all natural born innovators.

What we've managed to forget since then is how good it feels to express ourselves. But if every indigenous culture I've ever come across has this worked out, how did so much of the modern Western world forget?

Seriously: how did we put a handbrake on all this great creativity? How did we lose the ability to innovate that we all used to have in our souls? When did we start to squash this wonderful possibility framework that we're all hardwired with from birth? *What the hell happened?*

The way I hear and see it, many people can trace the loss back to a moment that happened somewhere between Years 4–7 at school.

It all started with a crappy comment for them. And I bet it did for you too.

It probably wasn't anything dramatic. In fact, it could have been something really small – a single thing someone said that stuck with you. Or it could have built up from a few little comments over the years. Either way, it finally convinced you that you weren't creative. And whichever situation is true for you, the end result is the same for everyone.

My most revealing insight into the effects of those crappy comments has come from a creative program called Team Masterpiece. I've delivered this program many times – probably around 150–200 times – over the last eight years. I've delivered it to a great mix of people too, from CEOs and executive teams through to sales, HR and EAs.

Basically, Team Masterpiece enables a team to create a fantastic painting that explores a theme and brings a story to life. The story could be a strategy, set of values, or visual of what innovation looks like for that team. I love this program, because teams always create something amazing, which blows everyone away. And the process we go through ties beautifully into innovation.

Without exception, everyone absolutely bricks themselves at the start of this program. Not a little bit, but a whole lot. Fear-wise, I'd put painting in the same basket as bungie jumping while letting a big, hairy spider walk over your face and wild rats run around in your underpants. There might not be any physical challenge to it, but mentally? Watch out!

That mental challenge is almost always driven by a crappy comment – usually one delivered by a teacher (often an art teacher) in those Year 4–7 classes. Look, I'm not dissing art teachers. After all, I used to be one. It's just that I see and hear this play out time and time again.

The crappy comment probably went something along the lines of, "Hmmm, your drawing is pretty average, Glen." Or "That looks nothing like a horse, Fran. Maybe you should choose Geography next year."

OUR
brains are designed to make creativity happen.

It's only a single, tiny comment – yet everyone I work with can remember hearing one like it was yesterday. It cut deep, and it stayed long.

The reason we remember it so well is that from that moment, we started to tell ourselves a different story to the one we told when we created castles. Right then and there, the possibility mindset that existed when we built cardboard rocket ships just a few years beforehand simply shrivelled up and died.

That crappy comment hangs like a weight around people's necks. It develops into, "You can't draw. You don't have a creative bone in your body. *You just aren't creative.*" It follows people through high school, then university, and finally into the workplace. It creates a really crappy mindset, which is the biggest disabler of creative potential that I know.

This mindset is ridiculous. Drawing is a learnt skill, but people equate their creative abilities with their ability to draw. Drawing is like personal finance or changing a car tyre: it can be learned and mastered. Creative potential, on the other hand, is something soul deep. It's simply part of who we are.

Unfortunately, the crappy "I'm not creative" mindset persists, driving our behaviour and actions for the rest of our lives.

The "I'm not creative" mindset in the wild

On a recent creative project, I collaborated with an agency to create some interactive visuals for a large financial company. We worked in the company's foyer as part of a larger communication rollout. We set up a board, and got everyone to write a word about something they found inspirational on the board as they walked past.

The idea was that the company would use this board as an ongoing communication piece in a bunch of different ways.

We set ourselves up in the foyer of two different offices over two days. On Day 1, people started off a little apprehensive, but quickly warmed to the task. On Day 2, though, it was almost impossible to get anyone to write anything on the board.

Most of them wouldn't even make eye contact. Before I'd even said anything, people put their heads down and said, "No, no, I can't do that – I'm not creative". They wouldn't – maybe even felt like they couldn't – write a single word.

And this was in a company that was known and revered for its great innovative culture too.

At the time, I couldn't help but wonder what the block was? Why were people so terrified of writing a word? This was their workplace: it wasn't like they were out in public. And they didn't have to start a blank canvas either: we'd done that for them. Again, there were no judgements or restrictions.

But the most troubling question was that if they said "No" to this when they should be saying "Yes", what else were they saying "No" to?

Now, of course, I understand that the Day 2 people almost certainly had the classic, crappy "You're not creative" comment from their pasts at play.

Refusing to write on the board was the simply external signs of their huge internal shit-fight.

It was all down to something that I like to call "the Ogre"

The Ogre is a creature that lives in *everyone's* minds. It likes to be heard, and it needs to be faced if you want any innovation on your horizon.

The Ogre is a bit of an arsehole. It's in the business of squashing any creativity you show, regardless of how you show it. It's the internal voice that says your ideas are a bit shit, so you'd better keep quiet about them. "Don't mention the inspiration you had when you were jogging," it says. "Don't share the quirky random thought either. And definitely, *definitely* don't share anything that could be innovative. You don't want to look stupid, do you?"

I'll talk more about the Ogre in Chapter 7, including how to dance with it so that it doesn't derail your drive for innovation. For now, though, let's look at a process I've developed to kickstart a culture of innovation in your organisation.

Imagine a ping pong ball on crack in a funnel (Welcome to the Framework)

"I have the answer!" screams the motivational speaker from the stage, sending the crowd of 15,000 into a wild frenzy. "My eleven-step process will completely transform your world!"

The answer immediately flashes onto the screen. It's there – and all for the *low, low* price of ONE MILLION DOLLARS. The crowd can see it!

"Oh my, oh yes," they say. "Just look at that process. It truly *is* the answer." They raise their smart phones, clicking away to capture what's onscreen. Hurrah.

Everyone looks excitedly at each other. "This PowerPoint slide! It's saved us!"

I can't be the first person to groan mildly when I see yet another seven-step (or five-step, or ten-step) plan from a guru who promises to change my life, or work, or mind, or whatever.

THIS

Framework provides principles, guidelines and plenty of levers you can pull to shift the thinking and behaviour in your workplace.

I also can't be the only person who's learned that "the answer" is rarely that simple.

People and organisations are complex, living entities. They can't just be stuffed into a set of steps and made to perform like a well trained seal.

So if you're looking for an easy answer to innovation, I have some good news and some bad news. Which one would you like first? Let's start with…

The bad news is that in the world of innovation, there's no one particular, perfect answer. Innovation is alive. It has its own personality and style, and it takes many different paths. That means it's not linear; because – as we mentioned in Chapter 4 – people are at the heart of innovation, and *people* aren't linear.

Remember: people, not a set of sequential steps, drive innovation. With people's unique styles, personalities, and approaches, there's no concrete, set-in-stone answer that's foolproof for everyone. Things that work for some organisations and people just won't work for others.

BUT.

The good news is that the bad news isn't actually a problem. In fact, the bad news is what makes the whole process of innovation so very exciting.

In our quest to avoid failure and our desire for an instant solution, we often seek a quick how-to guide or methodology that does almost everything for us. Having a clear path to follow seems logical, and makes perfect sense. Why waste time?

So, keeping both types of news in mind, I've come up with a set of steps that can be your guide to creating a culture of innovation in your company.

Because there's no one perfect answer, this Framework isn't a rigid set of rules that you use to beat your people up with. Nor is it a prescriptive manifesto that you have to follow to the letter.

Either of those options would be self-defeating, because a set, unwavering methodology for innovation will fall flat. At least, it will unless there are some accompanying mindset changes along the way.

Those changes include developing internal traits like:

~ Always being curious

~ Being brave

~ Using your imagination before jumping into a solution

~ Seeking out multiple forms of brain stimulation

~ Taking action

~ Being agile enough to quickly change direction

And these traits, in turn, require a real shift in mindset and behaviour. Again, this is not a bad thing: new perspectives and avoiding "Business as Usual" behaviour is essential for great ideas, creativity and a culture of innovation.

My Framework takes all of this into consideration. It combines everything I've learnt from my polar opposite corporate and creative careers, and blends them together in the middle.

This Framework provides principles, guidelines and plenty of levers you can pull to shift the thinking and behaviour in your workplace. Note that only using one principle or lever on its own won't drive a culture of innovation. Creating that culture takes time, bravery and lots of practice – practice at both developing behaviours, and at quieting the Ogre (there it is again!) until it doesn't exist.

Think of my Framework as a funnel that contains a ping pong ball on crack. That means the ball is busy. It eventually moves down the funnel, but in the meantime, it pings all over the place.

The top of the funnel is deliberately wide, so it can fit a constant stream of idea fodder going into it. The ball frantically moves up, down and sideways; and unexpected things happen to it all the time. It's contained, though, and moving in the right direction; so the good stuff eventually comes out the bottom.

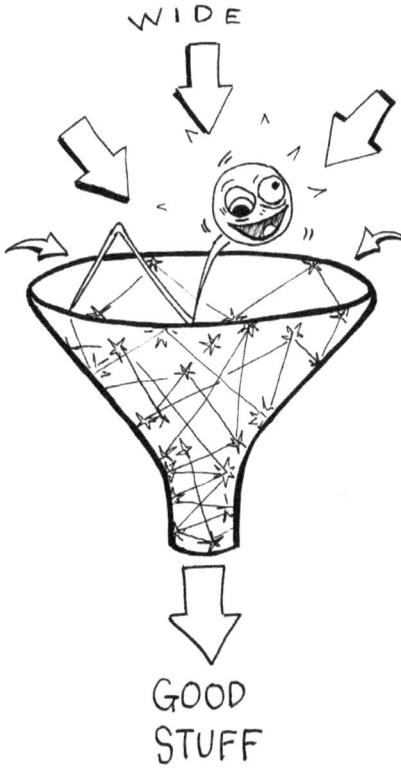

WIDE

GOOD
STUFF

Sound complicated? Don't worry. You're holding a handy guide-book to what's going on to help you through.

Whilst the Framework can't make you practice innovation, it *can* be a guide to fulfilling the innovation potential in your business. And it can definitely help you and your company to be a place where market-leading thinking thrives.

So, what does this Framework look like? I've listed out the steps in order below, but that's only because I have to (this is a book, after all).

What happens in reality, though, is that you'll start by sorting some initial mindset things out with your team, and then figure out exactly what problem you're solving. Then, chances are that you'll ping from one point to another as you start first to develop a culture of innovation; and then to develop solutions to your particular problems.

Then you'll repeat it all over again. It's an ongoing process, whose steps are:

1. **Dance with your Ogre.** This is where innovation often stops before it even begins! So acknowledge your monster. Get laughter happening, have some fun, and be ready for the challenge. Energy, fun, humour, and good vibes are all essential parts of the innovation process.

2. **Get your language right.** Many potential great ideas and products are killed by language the moment they're mentioned. Language drives thinking, which drives behaviour – and behaviour drives results. You need to replace the words "no" and "but" with "yes" and "and".

3. **So, what's the problem?** Innovation starts with a problem, not an idea. Get really clear on the problem you're trying to solve before you try to solve it. Keep asking "why?" to get to the heart of the issue, and keep focusing on the end user.

4. **Explore your idea.** Go really, really wide in your thinking before you go deep. Great stimulation in = great ideas out. To get really clear on what your problem is, leverage as many different approaches and styles as you can. Overload your senses with multiple forms of stimulation, and have some fun.

5. **Prototype and test it.** Get real with your idea and mock it up. Draw it out, cut and paste it, build it, make it visual, but whatever you do, create something tangible that people can interact with. Get real. What's working here? What's missing? Where would this stumble?

6. **Pitch it.** Every idea needs a commercial blowtorch applied to it. Get real, add some deadlines, and pitch. Be ready to tell people what's great about your idea, and embrace feedback and different perspectives.

7. **Repeat.** The process of innovation is never-ending. So you need a never-ending curiosity and energy to make great stuff happen. "Repeat" is the new mantra for a culture of innovation.

This Framework will not only enable you to develop great ideas. It will also help you to unleash the potential of the greatest asset you have in your business – your people.

Let's get started. Let's dive in and see what great ideas come out. Let's kickstart that culture of innovation, and get those thousand little lightbulbs all coming on at once in your business.

And yes, let's have some fun.

Framework #1: The internal shit fight with your monster

Let me introduce you to your creative Ogre. We all have one, myself included. So what is this Ogre? Think of it as a big, hairy monster that:

~ Always seems grumpy

~ Isn't nice to look at

~ Could be male or female

~ Pipes up whenever you try to do anything outside your comfort zone.

That last point is important to know, because the Ogre goes into overdrive whenever you go to do something that could be considered creative. At that point, its negative comments kick in:

> *"You're not creative. What you're doing will look, sound and feel like crap."*

And once those initial comments kick in, the rest are inevitable:

~ "You're no good at this."

~ "You'll fail at what you're doing."

~ "Someone may laugh at you."

~ And the clincher, "You're a very smart person. What you're doing may not make you look like the highly paid, intelligent professional that you are."

These negative comments are a big problem. They're a big problem for you personally; and also for companies that want to develop a culture of innovation.

Why? Well, how do you think it affects people who might share fresh thinking and creative ideas when their Ogres are constantly making these negative comments?

As you can imagine, the comments manifest themselves in those peoples' behaviours and outputs. For example:

~ You might suggest something that's left-field, then panic a little, and immediately crack a self-deprecating joke. Or the people around you might crack a joke, putting you down. In Australia's larrikin culture, this often happens at speed, and everyone joins in. "Ha, ha", they say, "You can't be serious, Smithy!" Either way, you shrink a little bit inside, but pass it off. And that's just want your Ogre wants you to do.

~ Something that requires creativity might come up; and you do it as half-heartedly as possible, giving it minimal effort. You don't care though. This creativity is just fluff, after all. It's kids' stuff.

~ When other people hear the word innovation, you notice them suddenly looking at their phones and dashing out of the room for an important email that they MUST deal with.

~ You find yourself thinking, "All this creativity and innovation stuff is for someone else. I'm a Leader. I'm a CFO (or an Engineer or an HR Specialist). I do very important stuff, so my job doesn't need this creativity crap."

People live the stories that their Ogres tell them. Those stories then become part of who they are.

The Ogre's story has a huge impact on innovation – and it has a huge impact on you as well. Your Ogre's voice is your own personal possibility thief. It's the story that stops you using half of the great brain function that you have.

Basically, as I said in the last chapter, your Ogre is an arsehole. It destroys so much of your good stuff. It steals a *huge* piece of what's possible for you, and then tells you that what it took doesn't matter. So you believe you lost nothing, and you don't even care.

You need to get real about your Ogre

Unless you (and the people in your team, and your wider organisation) deal with your respective Ogres, you will NEVER have a culture of innovation. It just won't happen. Seriously: I cannot stress how important this is. I'd stake every single thing I own on your need to deal with the Ogre before you can start an innovation journey.

I know people understand the concept of the Ogre, because I use it in every workshop I run. And at the end of those workshops, people always ask if they can keep their picture of the Ogre. There are images of that shit-stirring Ogre hanging in offices across the country to remind people of that crappy voice and what it tells them they can't do.

Now. If you're sitting there, thinking, "But I don't have an Ogre," congratulations. That's your Ogre talking to you now, trying to fool you. Trust me: we all have one. I deal with mine every day, and I do this stuff for a living. (Well, OK, my Ogre doesn't impact my creativity, but it's loud and clear in other parts of my life.)

The great news is that your Ogre's voice can be silenced. It can be tamed. One crappy comment from a teacher back at school doesn't have to smash your creative potential. It doesn't have to kill your capacity for fresh thinking and seeing more possibilities.

That comment doesn't have to crush your ability to drive an organisational culture of innovation and take great people with you either. You can smash your own Ogre and help your team members to smash theirs. You *can* have great ideas that constantly create market-leading thinking, products, and results.

That's why I see beating the Ogre as the very first step to kickstarting any type of innovation. Unless people change the negative stories about being uncreative that they've been telling themselves, nothing else will change. Innovation won't happen. Instead, the same-old-same-old stories and patterns will just keep repeating themselves.

Vincent Van Gogh said, "If you hear a voice within you say, 'You cannot paint,' then by all means paint, and that voice will be silenced." He knew of the creative Ogre and how to deal with it. He knew that the Ogre was (and still is) silenced by action. As with going for a walk, it all starts with taking a small step and repeating that action.

However, it's important to realise that overcoming the Ogre isn't a one-time thing. Yes, your Ogre will become quieter over time. But it's always worth checking in on it. Every day, ask yourself:

~ Is the Ogre speaking to me and limiting my creative potential?

~ Hang on, is the Ogre speaking to me in a disguised voice?

~ Am I hearing the Ogre in other people?

If the answer to any of these questions is yes, ask the Ogre out of its closet for a dance. Don't be surprised if it doesn't want to say yes: the Ogre doesn't like the light. In fact, nothing deflates it more than hearing you laugh at its comments, and discovering that you don't care as you continue to do great things.

So how do you get your Ogre out into the light, dancing a Tango with you? And if you're not a Tango fan, that's fine. You just need to move and act somehow.

That's why, in all the creative programs I run, people silence their Ogres with little steps of action. The main thing is to just get moving.

Action plus movement = results.

That's your mantra to kickstart a culture of innovation.

Think of it as like going for a long walk. You can talk about the walk you plan to go on. You can wonder about all the things you'll see on the way. You can look at a map of where you're going. You can have your kit all packed and ready to go. You can put on your new walking boots. You can open your door and look out to where you'll be heading. You can have regular meetings about the walk, and you can stretch and limber up.

But none of that actually gets you out of the door and walking.

Here's the deal.

Unless you take your first step, your walk will never start. You won't go anywhere. Once you get started and keep moving, though, things begin to happen. The walking becomes easier. After a while, you forget how hard it was to start. It becomes a completely natural thing to do.

I repeatedly see people struggling with this initial step though. There's a saying in marathon circles that when it comes to training runs, "The hardest distance of any run is the six feet between the couch and the front door". And that's just as true for long walks (and dealing with your Ogre).

Dances with Ogres: the documentary

One of the things I like to get people to do on any art and design program is to draw their name badge.

Why? This very small action starts them dealing with their Ogres. It lets people think about and choose colours in a safe way. It lets them create a small design with no one laughing. And it's a really easy way to engage their creative thinking by stealth.

When I run my Team Masterpiece program, one of my favourite parts is when I get teams to start drawing what their story or strategy looks like. Up until this stage, I've designed the program to be easy. There's lots of laughter and short, sharp, fun exercises to liberate their creative minds.

When I say that the next round of drawings will form the basis of their artwork, and that it will go on the walls of their offices, however, there's a noticeable shift in their demeanour. I watch their creative handbrakes come on.

That's where I remind each person about their Ogre and how to silence it. Here's how the process inevitably goes:

- *Each person grabs a crayon, then stares at their page as though it's going to bite them if they touch it. (Hello, Ogre.)*

- *They stare at their paper a whole lot longer. ("I'm going to look foolish.")*

- *Their hand hovers over the page, gliding back and forth. (More "Don't look foolish" thoughts.)*

- *Their hand makes a little mark on the page. ("Oh, shit! What have I done?")*

- *They make a longer line across the page. ("What the hell just happened?")*

- *They panic a little and look sideways at their team members. ("OMG, is anyone looking?")*

- *Some serious mind chatter starts up. ("Uh-oh, does theirs look better than mine?")*

- *Something moves internally, and they have an emotional shift. ("Hang on, this actually feels OK. I just felt something I don't think I felt since I was six.")*

- *More panic happens. ("OMG, I need to get a move on here. Simon's really pushing us.")*

- *A realisation takes place. ("This is going fine. I'm OK. This is… actually looking great.")*

- *The moment of breakthrough. ("Wait… the more I do this, the easier it gets. What Ogre?")*

- *The moment of triumph. ("Wow, look at my design! This looks slightly awesome!")*

- *A huge smile appears. ("This has been a load of fun.")*

Taking creative action then repeating it produces great results. You just have to suck it up at the beginning, and get stuck in.

Be aware

Make a note over the next few weeks of when your Ogre chips in and has a go at you, or when you see it in your team. Remember that the Ogre tries to hide itself by making you think it doesn't exist.

This is a great way to become aware of how often your Ogre tries to limit your potential. Whenever it does, smile, tell it to get stuffed, and move forward.

Over a few weeks, you should start to notice that your Ogre is yelling out less and less.

I see great parallels between silencing the Ogre and the adult colouring books that are so hot right now. Amazon's Best Seller list has been dominated by adult colouring books over the last few years. I've had long chats with my team and other artists about why they're so popular.

Our thoughts are that, quite apart from the mindfulness that these books encourage, we also all have a highly creative person inside us, just waiting to get out.

Adult colouring books allow us to experiment and express ourselves in a way that's safe – they're like a gateway drug for creativity. The drawings are already beautiful, and are so intricately drawn that they look amazing, no matter what colour combination we use. There are so many boundaries and guidelines to work within that the end result can't look bad.

Even though sketch books have been around for the last hundred years, they haven't been on the Best Seller list. Blank drawing books aren't as popular as adult colouring books, because blank pages are just too scary. If you tried making coloured marks on that blank page, your Ogre would start to scream at you about how crap your drawing was.

Adult colouring books are an example of how simply taking action and doing something can tame the Ogre. Its voice just can't be heard above the noise of experimenting, exploring, curiosity, and enjoyment.

Overcoming your Ogre and telling a different story around your creative potential is the very first step to developing a culture of innovation.

Dancing with your Ogre

Just before we head off and get excited about the Framework and what a culture of innovation can deliver, there are four principles to keep in mind when you're dealing with your Ogre. These things are vital to keep the innovation stream clear, and the ideas sparking happily.

When you embrace them, you force your Ogre to come out of its dark place where it can make its nasty comments. Out in the light, it can barely even whisper… (Poor Ogre. But happy you.)

Then, once it's in the light, you might want to see if it can dance that Tango.

A culture of innovation starts with a shift in behaviour and action.

Here are the four principles that will help you to make that happen…

1. Fail fast and experiment quickly

"There is no innovation and creativity without failure. Period." – Brene Brown

"Fail fast" has quickly become one of those go-to buzz words in corporate land. I haven't sat in many leaders' presentations lately without hearing some version of, "We need to fail fast, people." The phrase is up there with such classics as "Thinking outside the box" and "Drinking the Kool-Aid".

But… even though it may well be an overused cliché, it's still a great principle. And it's one that lies at the heart of the innovation process and design thinking.

I think this idea sits very nicely within the walls of Google, which I believe is where it started. Outside of Google, however, I think "fail" may not be the best word.

Why not? There are a few reasons...

1. **How many times have you heard the phrase "Failure is not an option?"**

   It's too easy to imagine a Navy officer screaming "Failure is NOT an option!" at his subordinates. His top lip curls up, and he snarls as his team sits there trembling. A small drip of slobber slowly falls to the floor. Splat. The team is paralysed with terror.

   Then two people slowly stand up. Of course. Only Iceman and Maverick could possibly have the heart for this mission. They alone can look possible failure in the eye and laugh (accompanied by epic soundtrack music).

2. **Obviously, you don't want everything you do to be a failure.**

   Try selling a business that isn't working, or that doesn't hit targets year on year.

"Don't worry," you say, "It's a great business. I've been failing for years." Who'd buy it?

3. **There's immense internal (and external) pressure not to fail.**

   Woolworths' foray into the home improvement sector with their Masters Home Improvement stores is a prominent Australian example of failing. No one wants to be the next Masters Home Improvement.

   That fear of failure can be stifling. Of course, the Ogre loves a fear of failure, because it's a certain creativity killer. "Don't try that," your Ogre says. "It may not work, and you'll look foolish. Get back in your very safe box, and let that idea slip away instead."

4. **The definition of "failure" is that something didn't work.**

   The dictionary says that failure is, "An act or instance of failing or proving unsuccessful; lack of success"[1]. The problem with this definition is that it doesn't give you a next step. Failure is the end result, so it's counter-intuitive to want to fail more.

In a culture of innovation, by contrast, failure has plenty of next steps. Failure isn't the end point: it's simply a springboard to greater learning.

Experiment quickly

In an organisation where fresh thinking, great ideas, and great products are normal, the concepts of "fail" and "fail fast" need a tweak.

Instead of "failing fast", I like the idea of "experimenting quickly". It just seems to conjure up a better experience. Would you rather be in a failure lab or an experimentation lab? Would you rather say, "Today I failed," or, "Today I experimented"?

I know that they're the same thing, but "experimenting" has an air of fun to it. "Failing" sounds like a dark place filled with ogres and trolls. Experimenting sounds like a happy, busy place where everyone runs around in white coats and crazy hairdos. There are fluffy, white clouds, and quite possibly bees buzzing about drinking little honey cappuccinos.

Spicing up your date night

Imagine that you and your partner have a date night, and you're the chef. You have a few different ideas in mind for the menu, and you want to channel your inner Jamie Oliver and use your creative flair.

As you dash off to the kitchen with a glass of red wine to make the meal, you say one of two things to your partner:

- *"Darling, I'm going to fail in the kitchen with tonight's dinner."*

- *"Darling, I'm going to experiment in the kitchen with tonight's dinner."*

Which one do you think would get a better response? Admittedly, anything with "kitchen" and "experimenting" in the same sentence may bring about a raised eyebrow, but you get the picture.

One of the great things that being an artist has taught me is that failure is OK.

As an artist, you're always experimenting and trying new things. You're constantly combining new materials and pushing to develop the style and variety of what you produce. You ask plenty of "What would happen if…?" questions.

This means that there are many, *many* failures along the way. Things break, don't stick, fall apart, turn out the wrong colour, and occasionally even explode. You don't set out to fail, but when you're constantly exploring new approaches, media, techniques, and styles, there are always things that don't work out as you'd imagined. An artist's job is being OK with that.

Anything that doesn't work out is *learning*, not failure.

My drawing portfolio is full of mistakes, but I've forced myself to keep all of my early art and drawings. Even though some were aesthetically unpleasing, they provide a great reference point for what I needed to improve on. My little fails have been a brilliant springboard to much better drawings. If I'd thrown away every drawing that wasn't working out, the learning from it would be gone too.

Just like art, the very nature of innovation involves unknowns. It has to. New combinations of ideas can only create unknowns. When you're operating at the edge of what's traditionally been done, you just don't know how things will turn out. There won't be any previous best practice case studies to follow.

So how do you find out what works? You experiment quickly on a small scale, and you learn from what happens.

With experimenting, there's no failure, only learning. Would the outcome of Masters Home Improvement have been different if there'd been plenty of little experiments and mini-fails along the way (all with subsequent learnings), rather than the very big, public fail at the end?

Remember: Failure = learning.

Roger Von Oech, the author of *A Whack on the Side of the Head* puts it well when he says, "Remember the two benefits of failure. First, if you do fail, you learn what doesn't work; and second, the failure gives you the opportunity to try a new approach."

Experiment quickly. Experiment on a small scale. Experiment often, learn from it, apply the learning, and repeat the process.

If your experiment works as intended, use the learnings and move forward. If the market gives you different feedback to what you'd imagined, use that feedback to create something better.

Because you do your experiments on a small scale, the implications of failure aren't huge. Your learnings, however, will be rich. Great improvements come from experimentation. Experimenting quickly is at the heart of innovation. It's also at the heart of responding to a rapidly changing market.

> *"If you're in this business and you don't expect failures or to get it wrong sometimes, you're never going to do anything significant." – Bill Maris, Google Ventures*

Try asking your team, "If we could experiment with one thing at work, what would it be?" I guarantee that you'll get a much better response than asking, "If we could fail at one thing, what would it be?"

Lots of little failures are OK, as long as you learn from them. In fact, they're what will put you on the path to success. That's why companies launch "minimum viable products" to market, and launch products in beta. It's done on a small scale with iterative feedback – I'll talk more about this kind of prototyping in Chapter 11.

2. When ideas come, write them down

I love the TV show Mad Men, based on life in a New York Advertising company in 1960s New York. There's an episode in Series 3 where copywriter Paul Kinsey is competing with former-copywriter and newly-promoted-creative Peggy Olsen for the creative work on an account. Paul's under a lot of pressure of his own making. He questions his potential and creativity, and worries what the Head of Creative, Don Draper, will think of him.

He's working late one night, drinking heavily, and spending some "me-time" in his office with a picture of Marilyn Monroe (those were the days). At around 2.30am, he wanders into the kitchen and starts talking to the cleaner, Achilles, and a great conversation unfolds. These events combine to spark the greatest idea Paul has ever had. He's jumping and screaming, his face lighting up, and he thanks the cleaner profusely.

ENERGY
impacts productivity (AKA "getting shit done").

Then he heads back to his office, and collapses on the couch with another whiskey, happy that he has something great. He's been saved… until, in the next scene, he's woken up the following morning on the same couch by his secretary. He starts frantically searching for that idea through the mess of his office. He accuses the secretary of taking his stuff, and just can't find the idea.

The story ends with Paul chatting to Peggy, his co-collaborator/in-house competition, lamenting the fact that he just didn't write his idea down. When he owns up to Don Draper, he even has Don's sympathy. There is true empathy from his colleagues: they understand the pain of what's happened.

In a culture of innovation, you'll have a thousand little lightbulb moments all the time. Recording those moments is essential. It's also a great way to brain dump. But most importantly, it stops you being like Paul Kinsey, and forgetting your good stuff.

How do you record those moments?

It's simple – and you already do it in other areas of your life. If you go into a meeting, you take notes and then use those notes later on. That stops you forgetting what was said in the meeting.
It seems so easy and normal in a meeting context, but we so often ignore the approach when it comes to great ideas.

So what's the best way to record your thoughts? There's really no right or wrong way. The aim is to just get them recorded. Here's what I do.

~ I record a huge amount of audio notes on my phone. For example, I listen to podcasts when I'm at the gym, which trigger many ideas. Speaking into my phone is a great way to record these ideas.

~ I have sticky notes everywhere in my office.

~ I have a large book with plain, white pages that I draw and record ideas in all the time.

~ I have another little pocket notebook that I take everywhere.

~ I take photos.

~ I pin ideas from magazines onto a cork board.

~ I use Evernote.

~ I take notes on my phone.

Our phones can be a great distraction, but they're also a great resource for collecting ideas. It's very rare that we don't have our phones with us. There are some great apps you can use to record and collate your thoughts and inspirations, including Evernote, which I mentioned above.

I run a lot of improvisation and storytelling programs with teams. When they're thinking up a scene or an idea to act out, I always tell them to write absolutely everything down.

I regularly see teams who are initially having a hilarious discussion with loads of laughter over 15 minutes. But when I then ask what ideas they had, I just get a load of umms and ahhs. They had lots of ideas: they just didn't write those ideas down for easy recall.

This is exactly what the Ogre wants: if you forget your best ideas, you don't have to take any action. Don't let it win. It's better to have 50 ideas that you can choose between, rather than lots of smiles but nothing that you can remember.

How else can you collect and record your thoughts?

The power of journaling goes beyond just writing down ideas: it also includes mindfulness, healing, stress reduction, and goal setting.

Like many creators, I just like to write and let the words free flow. Journaling first thing in the morning works best, as my mind has rested overnight, freeing up my subconscious. Is what I write always brilliant? Absolutely not, but allowing yourself to write in solitude, alone with your thoughts is a great way to explore what's floating around in your mind.

I always get insight when I discipline myself to journal often and early. Julia Cameron, who wrote *The Artist's Way*, calls this "Morning Pages". Her advice is to handwrite three A4 pages, and just dump whatever's in your mind. I go for two pages, but my advice is that anything written down is better than nothing written down.

Like any new habit, journaling regularly can take a little time. Keep at it, and the impact on your ideas and access to your subconscious will be phenomenal.

Another great way to collaborate and record ideas is to create and constantly add to a "Visual Mood Board": a collection of ideas and inspirations. This can be a pin board, a sticky note wall, or a whiteboard used specifically for ideas for your project. Cut things out and stick them up. Rip things, take photos, and write notes. Keep it rough and ready, but alive with inspiration. A Visual Mood Board also stimulates you to shift your thinking. Keep it changing and front and centre of your workspace where you can take action on it.

A culture of innovation starts with a shift in behaviour and action. Remember: great ideas happen all day, every day. A culture of innovation records them. Once ideas are hidden or forgotten, they're lost.

If you think it, record it. It's that simple. Don't be the person who says, "I had an idea once. What was it? I can't remember…."

3. Movement and Energy

I believe that energy is one of the most important parts of a culture of innovation, despite so often being overlooked. A culture of innovation shouldn't be hard to maintain; and keeping an eye on your energy by moving each day should be – and can be – straightforward.

Think about it. If you walk into a party, an office or a conversation, you can pick up on the energy straight way. I don't think there's a scientific way to measure that energy, but you certainly know when it's not there.

I believe that both good and bad energy can be contagious. If there's loads of good energy and a great vibe, they'll spread. If there's bad energy, though, watch out – because that can spread as well.

So, how does movement affect your ideas?

Energy has a huge influence on many things, not just ideas and a culture of innovation. Energy impacts productivity (AKA "getting shit done"), relationships, family, weekends, and overall happiness. You name it, your energy impacts it.

In the movie *Austin Powers: The Spy Who Shagged Me*, Austin Powers called energy his "mojo". Energy is the buzz or zest for life that we all have, and we mostly want more of. It's all the good stuff that we feel inside. It's what keeps us standing up, and ready to make good things happen.

If you're highly stressed or anxious, your brain follows its evolutionary trail back to caveman times, and goes into fight or flight mode. Imagine you're being chased by a sabre-toothed tiger. In that situation, there are only two good options: run, or fight. In a corporate world, however – especially one where you want to create a culture of innovation – two options just don't cut it.

When you're feeling the good vibes, on the other hand, your brain can relax. When that happens, you have more choices and you can focus better. Your brain releases dopamine – one of the feel-good neurotransmitters. Dopamine makes you feel pleasant and more motivated, and when you're in that state, your brain is open to plenty of choices.

But aren't creative people always a bit melancholy?

Literature and film (and maybe the odd real-life example) have given us the stereotype of an unhealthy, morose artist. We imagine someone who's lost in a world of despair, ripped apart by their creative struggles.

I want to paint a new picture for you – one of a creator who's filled with energy and good health. Someone who makes great things happen with their freshness and great vibe. Someone who's constantly moving. Someone who makes innovation thrive.

Unfortunately, movement isn't part of most people's day. My doctor was telling me recently that Australians aren't the active population that we're seen as being around the world.

We get up, and drive to work in the caves of our cars. We spend our days with little or no movement in the caves of our work. Then we drive back home in our car caves, and go from there into our house caves. We don't get any sunlight, and we spend between 7–14 hours of each day sitting. This is NOT a great recipe for inspirational thinking or great energy.

So what are some really easy ways to boost your energy? Apart from eating well and drinking plenty of water, try to:

~   Get outside for five minutes and have a walk (fresh air is your fresh thinking friend!)

~   Schedule some exercise in the middle of the day

~   Get a stand-up desk

~   Stretch a little

~   Do a few star jumps (if you have some privacy, or you just don't care)

~   Just stop sitting (you really don't need a guide for this)

I'm a fan of moving every hour or so, but this will be different for everyone. There are theories on how often to move, and the best amount of time to concentrate on one task. Techniques such as Pomodoro focus on working in 25-minute slots. Others suggest 52 minutes, or 90. Some people work through the night and get their best work done at 3am. If you find yourself in the zone, there's no point in breaking that creative flow.

The most important thing is to constantly check in with your energy and your creative flow. Know what your warning signs are, and watch out for them. Know when your energy starts to wane and your grey matter starts to cloud.

If you notice you're zoning out, move.

In the great book *Breakthrough! Overcome Creative Block and Spark your Imagination*, author Alex Cornell interviews 91 people, including:

~ Designers
~ Architects
~ Illustrators
~ Writers
~ Photographers
~ Film makers
~ Musicians

He asks them how they break through their creative blocks. Of the 91, approximately 80% listed movement as part of their routine to keep great ideas flowing.

I also recently listened to a video blog by hugely successful photographer Chase Jarvis about energy. His question was, "What are you doing wrong today that you could immediately put right tomorrow?" If you think about your movement and energy, chances are very high that you could change a whole lot of things immediately.

When I'm not on the road, I surf or swim in the ocean pretty much every day, even in winter. It's a habit I've developed over the last

20 years. I always have one of two discussions as I come out of the water in the winter and hit the showers on the beach.

Chat 1 (with someone fully clothed): *"You're mad, you are. I don't know why you do it. Brrrrrrr."*

Chat 2 (with another swimmer or water enthusiast): *"Isn't it great? You never feel bad when you get out." And we skip off up the beach together.*

It's the same with exercise and movement. No matter how hard it may initially be to get started, unless you break a leg or slip a disc in your back, you always feel better afterwards.

In a culture of innovation, moving is one of the quickest and easiest things to master. And, as a bonus, it kicks the Ogre right out of your head. (The Ogre is also a lazy bastard, and doesn't like the good vibes that movement creates.)

So check in regularly and start moving. Do something every hour. Put a spring back in your step, and a smile on your face. Watch the good energy flow and your imagination open up.

4. It's OK to enjoy yourself

Does life really have to be so serious? When did work become the land of the long, long face?

Yes, you have a very important, highly stressful job with extremely high expectations. You want to leave a legacy, and you want to make a real difference. So you can't spend every day in a state of frivolousness. But, on the flip side, do you really need to constantly maintain a serious demeanour?

Prima ballerina Dame Margot Fonteyn said, "Take your work seriously, but never yourself." Or in other words, "The result is important, but have some fun along the way too."

Just because something is fun doesn't mean that it's not useful.

Innovation and the creative process can – and should – be fun. It feels good to create. Deep inside you, there's a reservoir of creativity that needs to be expressed. There's a mountain of potential that you and your team are sitting on – and it feels amazing when you fulfil that potential.

Allowing yourself to enjoy the process of unleashing your creativity means allowing yourself to be human. Be OK with having fun with the imagination you've kept locked away until now.

Incidentally, it's no wonder that creative expression feels good. A 2016 study by the University of Otago found that everyday creative activity may lead to an upward spiral of increased wellbeing and creativity[2]. Their findings highlight an emerging emphasis on everyday creativity as a way to cultivate positive psychological functioning (i.e. feeling happiness and wellbeing).

Give your team permission to have fun with innovation. The Ogre likes people to have a bad time innovating and connecting with their creative selves. The moment people don't enjoy something, they tend to stop doing it (and fair enough too!)

It's much like how, after taking a long break from exercise, the first week of running can feel pretty crap. However, you know that if you're surrounded by great people who support and push you, by Weeks 2 and 3, you'll start to see the benefits and feel good.

American President Franklin D. Roosevelt put it well when he said, "Happiness lies in the joy of achievement and the thrill of the creative effort."

Imagine that you've received a permission slip from someone saying its fine to enjoy yourself. Would that make you feel better about having fun?

Write those permission slips to your team. Tell them it's OK to enjoy this brave new world of innovation. Tell them that the good feeling they get inside from using their natural creativity doesn't make them any less professional at work. It's going to help them do great things.

Who said that life had to be so serious anyway?

Dance practice

Over the next four weeks:

- ***Wear your experimenter's hat.*** *Whether they're big, small, or tiny, record all of the things that didn't work out as you expected; and next to each one, write what the learnings were. That's where the gold is.*

- ***Record your thoughts.*** *Give permission for your mind to go for a wander. No matter how trivial, record what thoughts come into your head. Keep a record of anything that grabs your attention. At the end of the four weeks, go back and review all your musings and see what gems you've unearthed.*

- ***Track your energy.*** *Check in every hour and ask, "How are my mind and body feeling?" Make a note of the times of day when they feel low, and what your warning signs are. Make a plan for what movement you will do to shift that energy. Get ready to watch your energy and output go through the roof.*

- ***Check in with your happiness regularly.*** *Are you being overly serious for no reason at all? If so, take five, deep slow breaths, and smile with each one. That's an easy one.*

By this point, you should have a clear awareness of how to keep the Ogre quiet and stop it from limiting your creative potential. Now it's time to talk about something else that kills ideas in their tracks: language.

Framework #2:
Check your language

Language is very, very powerful. Words can either cut through us like a knife, or lift us up to great heights. When we're feeling down, a few kind words can make all the difference. Particular words that someone said, good or bad, can stay with us for a life time.

Words have a *huge* impact.

In particular, they have a massive impact on innovation and the idea process. Poorly chosen words are one of the biggest idea-killers around.

Author and legendary former Head of BBDO Advertising Charles H. Brower said, "A new idea is delicate. It can be killed by a sneer or a yawn; it can be stabbed to death by a joke or worried to death by a frown on the right person's brow."

The biggest-idea killers of all are two small words. They're seemingly harmless. If they were animals, they'd be the size of cute (but very nasty) little rabbits.

If you're serious about creating a culture of innovation, you need to remove these two words from your organisation's language.

The two words to avoid: "no" and "but"

Have you ever heard this conversation at a team meeting? Someone says, "I've been looking at our process, and I think I may have a way to improve on xxxxxx." All too often, the responses are:

~   "*No, but* we've tried that before."

~   "Yes, sounds good in theory, *but* it won't work."

~   "Yes, *but* we've always done it this way."

These phrases – the words "no" and "but" together – kill the conversation, and any creative thinking and possibilities with it. In the words of Benjamin Zander, the conductor of the Boston Philharmonic Orchestra and the author of *The Art of Possibility*, these two words make the conversation, "spiral downwards instead of upwards".

I read an article recently about the power of language. In it, author, journalist and Fast Company contributor Michael Grothaus interviewed Professor Bernard Roth, academic director, author and cofounder of Stanford University's design school. Roth said, "We often use 'but' in place of 'and'. This substitution is so common that it sounds correct. Unfortunately, it often has the effect of changing a neutral statement into a negative one."

In fact, it's like the words "no" and "but" have become so common-place that we forget we're even using them.

Some great lessons on this topic come from the world of Improv (Improvisational) Theatre. If you've ever seen an episode of *Whose Line is it Anyway?* or *Thank God You're Here*, you'll have seen Improv in action.

Improv Theatre is totally unscripted, so most – sometimes all – of what happens is unplanned. It's live, and the actors make up everything that happens in the moment. I was heavily involved in the drama club at university, which is where I first came across Improv. Now I love to introduce it to the companies I work with.

One of my favourite innovation-day kickoffs is the "Yes, and" exercise.

Here's how it works. First, people form into groups of three. One group member suggests that the group does something or throws out an idea; and the other two respond with three different rounds of answers.

~ In the first round, they say "No, but…"

~ In the second, they say "Yes, but…"

~ Finally, in the third, they say, "Yes, and…"

This is a fun exercise, which provides a great insight into the power of language. As you can imagine, the results of each response are pretty intuitive:

~ "No, but…" frustrates the hell out of everyone, and the conversation doesn't go anywhere.

~ "Yes, but…" is a lot noisier, as the positive affirmation (yes) drives up energy and the general feel-good factor. However, this response ultimately delivers the same result as "No, but…". The conversation doesn't go anywhere.

~ "Yes, and…", however, moves the idea or suggestion forward, so the conversation can start to spiral upwards.

JUST
remember
that language
is powerful.

Two basic rules stick with me from Improv Theatre:

~   Always build on what someone gives you.

~   Never block (i.e. refuse) ideas.

These two basic rules allow actors on television shows like the two I mentioned earlier to deliver a great scene. For example, in *Thank God You're Here!,* the performer walks out onto a stage, not knowing what they'll see. They're greeted by another performer saying, "Thank God you're here!" They then need to improvise, building on the information they're given – without blocking any of it – to create a generally hilarious scene.

The words "no" and "but" are blockers; and when you block an idea, you can't build on it.

"No" and "but" are the language of Kodak and BlackBerry:

~   "*No but* digital photography will never catch on."

~   "Yes, I appreciate what you're saying *but* digital will tear away at our market-leading product of film."

~   "Yes, I know times are changing, *but* I retire in a few years."

~   "Yes, there are other smart phones with a lot more options, *but* ours has a QWERTY keyboard."

~   "*No, but* that will cost too much money to prototype. We're market leaders, and don't need to change."

~   "*No, but* people love our product."

Just to be clear: I'm not saying you should avoid the words "no" and "but" completely. They serve a genuine purpose in the real world, and this isn't some version of the Jim Carrey movie *Liar, Liar* where you can only say "Yes". If someone asks for another four weeks off because they really need to catch up on *A Game of Thrones*, "No!" is totally appropriate.

Just remember that language is powerful. Your team can remember words for years; and a "no" or "but" from you can kill their ideas before they get off the ground. Remember too that the Ogre makes us very sensitive about our ideas, and looks for any opening to tell us how crap they are. When people hear "no" and "but" before they've even started to explain their thoughts, it's an invitation for their Ogre to pipe up, and a surefire creativity killer.

The language that you use in conversations with yourself is just as important. Have you ever come up with an idea or wanted to try something, then found the limiting language kicking in?

~   "*No, but* what if you look foolish?"

~   "*No, but* you can't do it."

~   "Yes, you have an idea, *but* who will listen?"

~   "Yes, you've been on the course, *but* that doesn't make you an expert."

~   "*No*, just no. Don't say anything."

"No" and "but" aren't the only words to avoid

A phrase doesn't have to contain "no" or "but" to block someone else's ideas. Other idea-killing phrases to watch out for include:

~   "We tried that ten years ago, and it didn't work."

~   "Uh-oh, Bob thought that as well. Remember Bob? What a mess!"

~   "I appreciate that you've just started, so you won't understand…"

~   "We're accountants, Esme. We're not paid to have great ideas."

~   "I don't have a creative bone in my body."

~   "We're not the type of company that takes risk that easily. I'll form a committee, send that idea for review, and get back to you in six months."

~   "That's just not the way we do things around here, Gregory."

~   "Mmmmm, I'm not sure how practical that would be…"

~ "Wait… that's not what my team usually does."

~ "You know our members don't like change, Susan."

~ "Hah, have you been smoking wacky-baccy again, Dave?"

For most organisations, avoiding "no" and "but" is a complete cultural shift in language. We're all naturally masters of paralysis by analysis, so it's easy for us to immediately see – and say – what won't work. I also think the Ogre likes to convince people that being negative makes them even more clever than they are.

"Oh yes, I saw the holes in that one straight away," we tell ourselves. "Hah, she didn't even have to fully explain it, clever me. What's the next idea I can massacre? Team, come here. I have ideas I want to kill with my cleverness."

Don't underestimate the power of language in a culture of innovation. It's time to take a stand and change your language to be more innovative. It's time to call out the "no"s and the "but"s. It's time to make conversations and ideas spiral upwards instead of downwards. And it's time to get rid of those phrases that crush both fresh thinking and peoples' creative souls.

Next time you hear an idea that challenges your status quo, just take a breather. Shift your conversation from, "No, that idea is really crap, and will never work," to "Yes, that's different. Tell me some more about your thought process."

It's a hard habit to break, so go easy on yourself if you don't remember all the time. Just keep at it. Get your language right, and watch as the thousand little lightbulb moments start to happen all the time.

Do the work

Check in with your internal dialogue. How many "no"s and "but"s do you use? Record how many times these responses appear. Do they drive your thinking upwards, or stop it in its tracks?

> *Over a week, call out all the "no" and "but" responses that you and your team hear in your interactions. Ensure your team doesn't let you off the hook.*
>
> *At the start of your meetings, decide which idea-limiting language and usual go-to responses you'll rule out. Write these somewhere obvious, so that everyone remembers. Make a list of possible counter-responses that can drive great conversations further to replace them.*
>
> *NOTE: this will probably feel weird. If so, embrace the weirdness, and remember: "Business as Usual" is NOT the new normal.*

Once you start paying attention, you'll probably encounter some interesting things. They'll likely show up as stumbling blocks or rocks in the road when you're setting out to innovate. Maybe you've always known they were around, or maybe they've just been whispered about in the corridors.

Either way, you'll almost certainly come up against...

Mindsets, myths and fables

There are a few common mindsets, myths and fables that you should be aware of when you head off into innovation wonderland. They lurk behind corners, waiting to jump out and ambush the unwary.

They probably won't all show up every time. You might see one on one day, and another on a different day. Some people might see several at once. And some are direct opposites of each other. Whatever combination you have wandering your organisation's hallways, it's best to know about them and be ready for them before you encounter them.

1. "We've heard all this bullshit before"

I've been lucky to work with a great variety of clients and companies over the last sixteen years. I've worked with CFOs, Partners,

Marketers, EAs, Team Leaders, Engineers, Accountants, Heads of Innovation and Sales Champions. And all of them were really, *really* smart people.

These very smart people heard a lot of "stuff" over the years from trainers, consultants, executive management, and their Global Head Office. They'd been through plenty of change programs and new initiatives. Whenever a new leader had started, the strategy and vision they brought with them mostly changed compared to whatever had been agreed just twelve months before.

And after a few too many years, these very smart people developed a bullshit radar through which all new information needed to pass before being judged. New restructures, executive decisions, changing leadership styles: it all contributed to the way their brain filed and labelled things; and it all continues to build that powerful radar for bullshit.

Fast forward to now, and pretty much any new initiative or change triggers it. The moment someone uses those words, their alarm bells sound. "Whoop, whoop, bullshit approaching, whoop, whoop!" Rightly or wrongly, it's there: "Whoop, whoop, whoop."

Whoop! Whoop
Whoop Whoop!

BS BULLSHIT ALARM

As someone who wants to kickstart a culture of innovation, you can't pretend that your people don't have these bullshit radars. You can't pretend the "Whoop, whoop, whoop," doesn't exist.

Realise that *anything* you say or do will have to pass through each team member's radar. And realise that, as such, you'll hear a variety of opinions when the word innovation is mentioned. Be prepared for it.

2. It feels uncomfortable

> *Life begins at the end of your comfort zone*
> *– Neale Donald Walsch*

Most of us *love* to spend time in our "comfort zones". As an example, we get home from work. We flop down on the couch, exhausted, in front of the TV to watch our favourite show. "Ahhhhh, here I am again," our brains think.

The couch is comfortable, and it's easy. Not much happens, granted, but it's a smooth, uncomplicated place.

The problem is that the best things always happen outside of our comfort zones. And if we feel any discomfort, then – like most people – we naturally stay away from whatever caused it.

The power of the comfort zone

I saw a great example of the power of the comfort zone recently.

We have a local beach that faces west just inside a headland. This means the water is calm and smooth, so it's a great place for small kids to swim. These same conditions make it great place for paddle boarding; and it's heavily visited by tourists and locals.

I was in the water with my young kids on a beautiful day, and I saw a woman in her early 40s, whose husband was encouraging her to have a go at paddle boarding. He'd just been for a paddle and was excited about it – and he really wanted his wife to experience some of his excitement.

On smooth water, you can get the hang of paddle boarding quickly. The woman stood up, and immediately fell off into the shallow water. This is totally normal; but for her, that was the end of it. Five seconds later, she said that she just didn't want to do it.

Of course, other people were falling off their paddle boards elsewhere. They didn't care. She cared though. Falling off felt uncomfortable; and because it was outside her comfort zone, it was enough for her to draw a line through what could be a great activity. Her husband kept encouraging her to stick with it, saying that she'd have a great time, but she steadfastly refused.

Having been through the same experience with paddle boarding and watching many others do the same, I suspected that if she'd stuck with it for even just ten minutes more, she'd have been successful. She might then have been able to share some of that great joy with her husband. She just needed to stretch a little further to find out, instead of stopping at the initial discomfort.

So what was the problem here? It wasn't her physical discomfort. It wasn't like she was being asked to eat a bag of worms in a TV show like *I'm a Celebrity, Get me Out of Here*; or walk barefoot over a hot, mid-summer bitumen road. It just felt uncomfortable internally.

The Ogre loves it when you get uncomfortable. It smiles contentedly, knowing your discomfort will snuff out yet more brilliant potential.

In a similar way, creativity and innovation have become something way outside of most people's comfort zones (and often, even in their panic zones).

Yet, great things happen when people push through the edge of their comfort zones and into their stretch zones. That's where growth and development live, and where people thrive – if they make the effort. The awesome thing is that the more you practice something, the more comfortable it becomes. Great things become easier to achieve.

As the American author Kurt Vonnegut put it, "I want to stay as close to the edge as I can without going over. Out on the edge, you see all kinds of things you can't see from the centre."

3. I love sport, not arty farty stuff

I can still remember when a potential client said this to me. It made me laugh at the time; but many people think the same way.

You could almost call this mindset an Australian classic, especially for the blokes. We live in a country where sport dominates. Now, make no mistake: I love sport. It keeps us fit, teaches us teamwork and life lessons, and helps us to develop great friends and social bonds.

In Australia, sport has a massive influence on our psyche. Sports stars dominate the speaking circuit, each with their own fascinating stories and metaphors around goal setting, motivation and achievement. Sport and its life lessons are revered throughout the corporate landscape.

I've actually worked with a couple of professional sporting teams whose members are at their physical peak, and driven at a level that's beyond most people's comprehension. They're elite athletes who all but run through walls in their training. And that's the psyche we're all encouraged to have in our workplaces – one where we *just smash it*.

But you know – the moment that I mention "creativity" (or if you dare, "art"), I get a very different response from these sporting behemoths.

That's why I always smile whenever I watch the, "I love sport, not arty farty stuff," play out. I've worked in very large art museums around the globe too, and here's what I see regularly happening…

A date at the gallery

Picture this: a couple is out on a romantic date at an art gallery. Craig (Smithy to his mates) has been taken there by his wife.

He's looking at a very large artwork, wondering what the hell it's all about. He doesn't dare to check the footy score on his phone – after all, this is a date. He looks around and sees another male, Macca, also looking at the same very large painting, and also on a date.

Craig and Macca nod at each other in silent acknowledgement. They know what the other one is going through. They look at the artwork, then slightly tilt their heads to peer at each other again. Then they nod in unison towards the picture, and both raise their eyebrows.

They slowly shuffle a little closer to each other, sideways like crabs. Finally, Craig speaks up. "What's this shit then?"

Macca replies, "A kid could paint this crap. I could paint this crap. I'm going to go home, paint a picture, put it on eBay, and sell it for one million dollars".

Both men nod vigorously at each other, put their hands in their pockets and walk aggressively away from the artwork. They immediately see their respective partners, smile, and feign sincere enjoyment as they look into their partners' bags to see what they got from the overpriced gift shop.

The Ogre loves these gallery visits. It's unfortunate, but for many, many people, art and galleries both fall into the "out of the immediate comfort zone" experiences.

A culture of innovation exists when people bring their most interesting and creative selves to work.

As you know, the Ogre loves it when people feel a little scared. One of the easiest ways for them to quickly push down this fear is to mock whatever they don't understand. This keeps them safe, and lets everyone know they don't give a shit. Once people start to mock something, their brains default to putting that thing in the "totally useless" file. And once something's in that file, it almost always stays there.

The problem is that for many people, art (which they don't understand and/or believe that they can't create) is the only way to measure their creativity. Ever since that crappy comment they heard when they were younger, they tell themselves that they aren't creative. They say things like:

~ "I can't draw – I don't have a creative bone in my body."

~ "Creativity is for all those arty farty types."

~ "I don't understand art – I'm not creative."

~ "Art is *the creative stuff other people do*."

Appreciating/creating art and being innovative are *two completely different things*. You don't need to understand art to be a great innovator. As with art, however, innovation does mean being open to engaging with things you don't immediately understand.

Innovation is a normal part of being human, but it's also a choice. It's a choice about how you think, and about how far you're willing to stretch yourself and be open to something you don't immediately understand. It's a choice to open your eyes and enjoy a journey of exploration. And it has nothing to do with whether or not you currently like – or understand – art.

So how do you solve this "engaging with art" dilemma? Just keep it simple and enjoyable, and remember that it's actually OK not to like something. That's the advice I give to my sport-mad Dad: just look at different types of art, and notice your reactions to it. If you like it, great. If not, that's fine as well. You don't have to like everything, and having a reaction is normal.

Also, enjoy the experience of your thinking being taken in a different direction for a few hours. This really throws the Ogre off as well: if you're just looking for, and then accepting, your own reactions, it has no idea what to do.

Maybe those trips to the gallery can be a little more enjoyable as well.

4. I'm secretly creative at home, but boring at work

I see this one a lot. People can have split personalities; and at home, under the cover of darkness, they just seem more inclined do creative things. For example:

~ They experiment in the kitchen.

~ They build things in the garden.

~ They read books and magazines.

~ They take photos.

~ They have quirky hobbies.

~ They organise amazing parties for their kids.

~ They plan fantastic holidays.

~ They design a home entertainment system from scratch.

These are all creative activities.

For some reason – maybe because there's nobody to see them – many people seem a lot more inclined to act like innovators at home. They leave their creative selves there, never revealing that side of themselves at work.

I recently worked with a risk team for a not-for-profit organisation. They were brilliant people and loads of fun. We were re-imagining how a new five-year plan might look, and discussing the new way of working and fresh thinking required to bring it to life.

As we talked about embracing a creative mindset, one of the participants said, "I'm the most uncreative person in the world."

I asked him what his hobbies were, and he replied, "Photography and cooking."

Of course, the room all laughed out loud: photography and cooking are both extremely creative hobbies. These activities give people a unique way of looking at things; and they exercised his brain in a way that naturally develops fresh thinking.

So here was this truly creative person who didn't acknowledge it; and as such, he couldn't bring any of that fresh thinking to work. His mindset was, "I work in risk, Simon, not the creative department." Yet that was exactly the type of thinking the team's new five-year plan needed.

And so he left far too much of his potential on the floor.

This "secretly creative at home, but boring at work" mindset needs to change. A culture of innovation exists when people bring their most interesting and creative selves to work. The mindset and behaviours that drive your team's quirky pursuits at home are absolutely essential for a culture of innovation at work. Originality, vibrancy, imagination, and curiosity are all transferable skills.

So stop being embarrassed that you used to play guitar when you were younger. Stop keeping quiet about your obsession with making the perfect cake. Stop hiding the fact that you're seriously into scrapbooking. And if you know five languages, studied Flamenco dancing in Spain, or have fifteen adult colouring books, shout about it from the roof tops!

Why don't people bring their best, most innovative selves to work? Why do only their boring sides turn up? You guessed it: it's the Ogre again. The Ogre focusses us on our fear of embarrassment, and our worry about teammates laughing or making classic put down comments. And so we take the easy route, and leave our more unique selves at home.

As I mentioned earlier, an essential part of innovation is trying new things, having fun, and creating some good energy. So your role as a leader is to create an environment for your team where fun, energy, and imagination thrive.

What are you waiting for? It's time for you *and* your team to bring your best selves to work.

5. *"What if I put my cap on backwards?"*

Sometimes people try to create a culture of innovation that doesn't… quite… fit.

They know they *want* change. They know they *want* a shift in culture. But the how of it is fuzzy. So they feel as though they need some kind of external marker to prove that innovation is really taking place.

They do the equivalent of putting their cap on backwards, and assume that a cascade of innovation will automatically follow.

Putting your hat on backwards doesn't equal creativity or a culture of innovation.

Let's picture a leader, and let's make him a man. He's done a recent leadership development course that included a module on innovation. He knows that everyone's speaking about this innovation stuff; and he understands the importance of market-leading thinking and great ideas.

Let's say this leader wants to stir things up a little. "That's what this place needs," he thinks. "A shakeup, some new ideas, and brainstorming". So he gets everyone together for a meeting, and sends out a note beforehand that says, "Expect something different."

When it's time for the meeting, he walks into the room with his cap on backwards. He figures he's sending a message that things are now hip, cool, creative, and innovative. They'll be different – just like his cap.

The problem is that, despite his best intentions, the backwards cap doesn't shake *anyone* up the right way. The audience doesn't think the cap is hip, cool, and creative. They just think their leader looks like a bit of a tool.

As a person with influence, you need to put yourselves in your audience's shoes. You need to realise that putting your hat on backwards, doing a moonwalk, or saying "groovy" a lot just doesn't work. Looking a little more casual and saying words like "brainstorming" or getting an air hockey table doesn't generally get a team excited about innovation either.

Instead, try just being real and genuine with your team. The innovation journey will produce plenty of surprises for everyone. So enjoy the trip, and just be who you are: someone who's probably as daunted by this whole innovation stuff as the team you lead, but ready and excited about the challenge.

You can leave your cap in your desk drawer (or at least put it on the right way).

6. Excuses

You're certain to encounter an excuse or three while you're kick-starting your innovation culture. It's the same all over: everyone has the best reason that innovation and creativity won't work in their industry, culture or organisation.

This is where your own bullshit meter should be going off.

Here are a few of the phrases that I hear regularly, which could be called the "Legacy Excuses":

~ "Simon, things move so slowly around here. That's just the way it is."

~ "The system we have set up just means that signoff takes over twelve months."

~ "We tried that once, and it didn't work."

~ "There are some people who really live in the past here." (Complete with eye roll).

~ "But that's just the way we've always done things around here."

~ "By the time we got it up and running, it was irrelevant."

~ "I'll just have to run that through our Singapore Office. They generally reply within two weeks."

~ "Our invoicing process takes three months to pay you." (I actually need to just let that one go…)

There's absolutely no doubt that the organisation you work for is a complex ecosystem, and a mosaic of challenges. And of course, the bigger your organisation, the more complex your challenges will be.

But I say, "No more excuses!" Screw all the legacy issues you've had. Do you want to be relevant in twelve months' time? People may not like change, but not-changing just isn't possible anymore. Digital disruption and super-savvy startups are gobbling up your market everywhere.

If that's going to change, *you'll* need to change it. *You* are the person who'll start creating your innovation culture from within, one step at a time.

Do the work

Just as in the exercise where you needed to notice whenever you used "no" and "but", I'm now asking you to notice when you're caught up in the mindsets, myths and fables I've outlined.

Have a really good think about this. Make a list of the particular mindsets and myths that play out in your day-to-day operations. Some may be really obvious, others not so much.

Share these with your team and your wider organisation. Importantly, ask if there are any you've missed. You may be involved in some that you aren't even aware of. (The Ogre's sneaky like that).

Note the patterns when they pop up, and be brave enough to call them out. Most importantly, make a plan for what you'll do to change them.

Don't be the last person in Excuse Town looking for company

Creating an anti-Ogre environment

Finally, a culture of innovation requires the right environment for quality people to shine and thrive. This is not unique to any one industry. If you want a great sales culture, you need to create the right environment for sales to thrive. If you want a culture of safety and want people to go home alive, you need to create the right training, resources and environment for this to happen.

This is where the Ogre loves to step in. He loves to kill a culture of creativity and innovation.

As I mentioned in Chapter 6, nothing great can happen until the Ogre is silent. That's why beating it is the very first step in my Framework, and checking your language is the second. Unless people change the negative story they've been telling themselves, nothing else will change; and a culture of innovation won't happen.

Meanwhile, if you have a creative culture with vibrant energy and great people, where everyone is kicking arse, there's no better place to be. That's why the next steps in this Framework will show you how to get both yourself and your team taking their innovation possibilities to an all-time high (and kicking a little arse in the process).

Framework #3: "So what's the problem?" asked the curious cat

Ok everyone, get ready: we're going to innovate now. First, though, let's make sure we're ready to go.

~ Dealt with the Ogre? Check!

~ Got our language in order? Check!

OK, we're ready to fire. Hang on, what are we going to innovate *about?*

(For what it's worth, an answer of "Don't worry, team. Just be innovative about anything. Everyone's doing it," doesn't actually start the innovation process off well.)

Innovation starts with a problem, not an idea

Before you can innovate, you must be really clear on the problem you're trying to solve. Not just "a little" clear, either; but *completely* crystal clear. Hopefully, I'm being really clear there myself.

At this point, you need to be a curious cat. (Side note: I don't believe that curiosity ever killed the cat. I think curiosity made it a pretty amazing feline. And when the cat combined curiosity with great information, it became Supercat.) You need plenty of both curiosity *and* information to work out what the problem is.

Asking, "So what's the problem?" provides clarity, structure, purpose, and direction. It also gives you empathy and understanding for the people whose problem you're trying to solve.

I like the way that Aleem Walij talks about this. Walij is a social innovator, former Chief Innovation Officer within the World Bank, and now head of the Agha Khan Foundation, USA. As he puts it, "Don't be an answer looking for a problem." Define the problem first; *then* work with your users to solve that problem.

Who has the answers to the problems you need to solve? Your *market* and your *customers*. Chances are that if you ask your market good questions, you'll get good answers. If you and your team ask yourselves good questions, you'll probably get good answers and plenty of great insight.

What are some of the key questions you should be asking?

~ Who, exactly, is our customer?

~ What are our customers experiencing right now?

~ What pains are our customers having?

~ What's causing our customers' behaviour?

~ Have we asked our customers about this?

~ What do our customers want to experience?

~ What are we really trying to achieve, and what problem will that solve?

~ Why is it important to solve this problem?

~ How do we know we're solving the right problem?

~ Why are we exploring this?

~ How will we know we've been successful?

~ What's the meaning of my life? (Just joking, that's for my next book.)

This is the time to be very detailed, and develop a clear statement of your problem. It's essential to find the root cause of your problem, so that solving it will have the biggest impact. This isn't a time for fluffiness; and in my experience, this can be tough. Once you've developed your problem statement, however, the problem you're solving moves to front and centre for everyone who's working on it.

I'm a fan of making your problem statement a question. A sample problem statement/question could read something like, "How do we create a new approach to X, so that our customers will experience Y, and will therefore be able to achieve Z?"

Great innovation comes from putting the end user at the heart and soul of the process. It's very easy to get excited about fixing something that isn't a problem, and then design a solution that nobody needs.

BEFORE

you can innovate, you must be really clear on the problem you're trying to solve.

The taxi industry is going through some challenges that have been brought on by a non-user-centred approach. As a rule, customers didn't like:

~   A 5–10% credit card surcharge on their trip

~   High prices

~   Dirty taxis that smelled and weren't enjoyable to be in

~   Grumpy drivers

~   Most importantly, not being able to find a taxi when they needed one

A sceptic might say that the problem the taxi industry was trying to solve was "how to make as much money as possible". That problem statement wasn't about solving a customer's problem, however. From the customer's perspective, the problem is more like, "How can I get a taxi at 3pm, when all the drivers are changing shifts?"

Would Uber have been able to disrupt the way they did if the taxi industry had been trying to solve the customer problem of, "How do I get from point A to point B in the safest, most cost-effective and convenient way possible?"

My guess is "no", since they'd have had far fewer unhappy customers in the market.

Always keep asking "Why?"

Einstein said, "It's important to never stop questioning." And that's *exactly* the approach you need to take.

One way to incorporate this into your organisation is to work with the "Five Whys". These were made famous by Sakichi Toyoda, and used within Toyota Motors to help it become the powerhouse it is today.

To use this technique, you need to ask "Why?" in response to a statement of the problem you're having. Keep asking why for each answer, until you've asked (at least) five times. This will bring you to the very core problem, every time. If you don't feel you're quite there yet, just ask "Why?" again.

Example 1

~ Our team is spending around 25% longer this year to complete projects. Why?

~ We're spending time too much time in meetings. Why?

~ We've had a huge number of new arrivals. Why?

~ The company has grown rapidly, and new arrivals don't understand the complexity of what we're doing. Why?

~ We have an inefficient onboarding program. (This is the real problem.)

Now that you've defined your problem – an inefficient onboarding program – you have a definite direction for your innovation to head in.

Your team can then start exploring and prototyping ways to make your onboarding program more effective, so that new people hit the ground running (rather than walking in a circle, flapping their arms, and hoping for the best).

Example 2

~ I don't feel fit anymore. Why?

~ I don't exercise in the mornings like I used to. Why?

~ I wake up tired every day. Why?

~ I drink too much in the evenings? Why?

~ I'm always attending work functions, and the alcohol is free. (This is the real problem.)

Through the process of asking why, the problem of not feeling fit completely shifts. You have a much clearer direction from which to solve your problem; and the range of solutions will address the real problem, not the surface one. Possible solutions focus on working out ways to say no to some work functions, having a pre-planned exit strategy at 7:30pm, or reaching for the Lemon, Lime and Bitters.

Constantly ask why, and stay curious. It's better to ask a seemingly stupid question up front, rather than not ask that question and look stupid later on when you're solving the wrong problem.

Ask "Why?"

Think of a problem you or your team are having, or an area where you just feel stuck. It should be something that you want to shift, but where not much has been happening.

Make a statement about that problem, and write it down on paper.

At the end of the problem statement, write, "Why?" Then, on the next line, answer that question.

Run your statement through a series of "Why?" questions, until you're at the heart of the problem. Don't feel that you have to stop at five. Keep going until you feel you've reached the root cause.

When you get to the heart of the problem, you can then start working on ways to address it. Chances are that the problem may be very different to what you thought it was.

It's OK to ask far more questions than everyone else. It's much easier to innovate once you get really, really clear on the problem you need to solve.

Remember that great questions produce great answers (and innovative solutions). Oprah Winfrey said, "Ask the right questions, and the answers will always reveal themselves". Who argues with Oprah? Not this curious cat.

Not all problems have to be hard to solve. You just have to focus with surgical precision in the right place. Don't be happy with the first answer that comes up. Listen to and understand your users and their problems

Most of all? Don't be an answer looking for a problem.

Framework #4: Explore your idea – the miniseries

PART 1 – PRE-CAFFEINE

(A quick note for the goldfish minds out there: if you're like me, you probably need regular breaks when you have to take in a lot of information. And, perhaps appropriately for the widest part of the funnel, this is the longest chapter of the book. So to give you a chance to take a coffee-break at the midway point, I've split it into two. For the moment, just buckle in, and get ready for an epic chapter – I'll let you know when it's time for that tasty brew.)

Remember that innovation funnel I mentioned back in Chapter 6? The one with the ping pong ball on crack bouncing around in it? Well, the space at the top of your funnel is all about exploring your idea.

In my experience, this is where large companies always struggle the most. To get quality innovation, you *must* have a constant stream of fresh thinking about the problem you want to solve for your clients. That's why the funnel is extra big at the top. That way, there's plenty of room to fill it with ideas that produce great products and services at the other end. The trick to filling your innovation funnel is to allow yourself and your team time to *explore* your idea (or ideas).

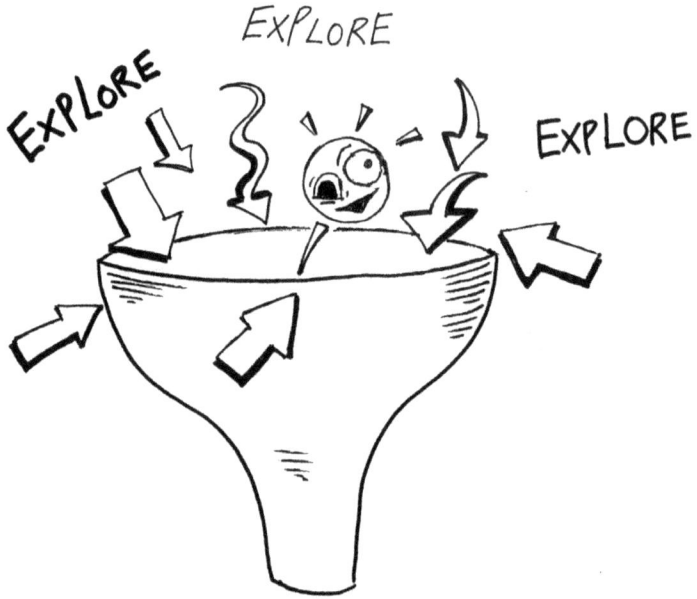

Why is that so tricky? Well, analysing an idea and its *lack* of merits is easy. You can shred an idea and pull it apart in a moment, like a flock of seagulls going after a bag of hot chips at the beach. That behaviour of immediately seeing why something *won't* work comes much more naturally to most people than exploring how it *might* work.

Perhaps that's why many large organisations struggle to get ideas in the first place. It's hard work to keep fresh thinking coming in thick and fast. Instead, most companies operate in the land of the long, blank face and the white, blank page. The land of "Let's just check the mobile one more time". The land of "Please don't look at me anyone".

We don't tend to hear about the process of generating and explor-ing ideas in all the usual innovation stories. Those stories mostly focus on successful end products, all-but ignoring everything else that happened along the way.

Over the last few years, I've struggled to hear a presentation from a senior leader that doesn't reflect this focus. "Ohhh," they enthuse. "Let's talk about Uber. They're so innovative, fresh, and disruptive. Let's Uber-ise."

There's a good reason those leaders keep referring to Uber. After all, the company has pretty much nailed innovation. It found a market where customers were unhappy, and disrupted that market to help make them happy.

Here's what you *don't* hear in those presentations, though:

~ Uber would have had many struggles along the way.

~ They probably explored hundreds of ideas in the process of coming up with the one they're best known for.

~ They almost certainly didn't write two ideas on a flipchart, then say, "Perfect, that's done!" and move to the next task.

~ They would have looked far and wide in the process, then further and wider, and then further and wider after that.

~ Their great ideas probably didn't all happen around a boardroom table.

~ Their product certainly didn't happen overnight.

~ They probably had multiple forms of stimulation feeding in to help them put the idea together.

~ They no doubt kept at it with relentless enthusiasm and energy until they got there.

~ They would have celebrated little wins along the way.

~ They probably used the many mistakes they made as gold nuggets of learning.

~ They would have needed to keep their thinking fresh and seek continuous stimulation.

~ They almost certainly kept coming back to, and exploring, their end user's experience.

YOU

don't grab new market share with the thinking of five years ago.

~   They probably constantly experimented and tested different ideas with their market.

~   They would have explored their idea from multiple angles to give them a greater understanding of both their drivers' and customers' needs.

~   They definitely didn't get it right the first time.

~   They had to push through any Ogres they encountered.

~   They probably had a very wide idea funnel that they constantly filled.

~   They would have embraced other people's ideas and feedback as the team developed.

~   They definitely didn't throw their hands up and say, "Screw this, I'm giving up!" the first time there was a hiccup.

To get to the point where they were the example in every leader's presentation on innovation, Uber would have explored ideas and kept *on* exploring them. They would have mashed the ideas about, created many iterations, tested them, learnt, added more fresh thinking, and then done it all again.

(Of course, given Uber's recent issues with culture and behaviour, they may start to appear a little less in presentations.)

I imagine that this approach will be a constant feature of a company like Uber. You don't disrupt a market with Business as Usual (BAU) thinking. You don't grab new market share with the thinking of five years ago. You won't even *maintain* market share with last year's thinking.

How do you keep your thinking fresh?

There are many, many ways to explore ideas and develop fresh thinking. Most of them are actually kind of fun if you lean into the process, enjoy it, and let it energise you. Rest assured: BAU thinking will always be there when you need it. For now, let yourself get a tiny bit excited about new possibilities.

In an interview with Forbes Magazine, Laszlo Bock, Senior Vice President of Google's People Operations said, "We try to have as many channels for expression as we can, recognising that different people, and different ideas, will percolate up in different ways"

It will be the same for you and your organisation. The right combination of approaches to throw into the mixing pot will be different for everyone. This is not a "my way or the highway" situation.

Additionally, the sequence of developing ideas will chop and change, grow, develop, and produce unexpected turns at every corner. Those ideas probably won't follow the sequence that you originally had in mind. Their start and finish points will be fluid. Things will happen that are unique to your team, your great energy, and the experiences that brought your team to where they are.

Just get stuck in. Productivity always beats perfection at the idea exploration stage. The very nature of initial ideas is that they aren't perfect. That's why you move them through the Framework to improve them. The problem in so many companies is that they throw ideas to the wolves long before they should.

Remember that market-leading thinking comes from exploring different ways to solve problems. A culture of innovation comes from exploring ways to help your market. That's why constant exploration is essential for developing a stream of great ideas, products, services, and results.

Put on your exploration hat. It's time to take your mind for a wander.

Great things in = great things out

The No.1 thing you need to remember with developing great ideas and market-leading thinking is:

Great things in = great things out.

Brilliant chefs, artists, designers, architects, and authors have all known this for years.

Every time you open a book, read a report, or connect with new people and have a conversation, you take in new things. The same is true when you go somewhere different, or experience something new. You allow in much more information. That helps you to create new files, and gives you somewhere to go outside of your usual filing system when you're next required to think differently.

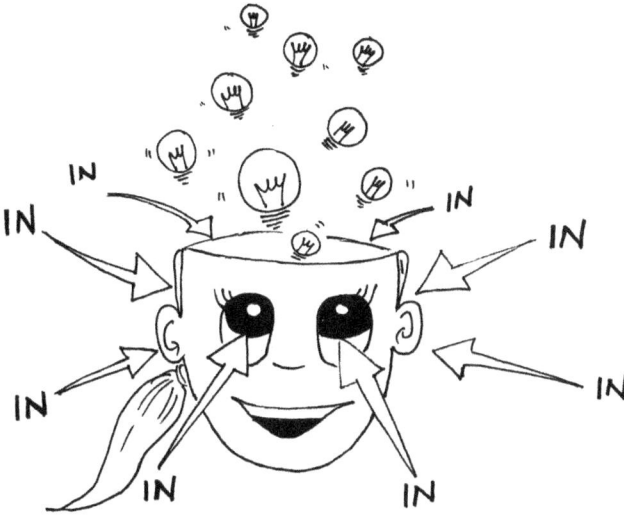

Let's compare two people to see how much difference this can make:

~ **Robert:** Robert has held the same job for 30 years, and takes the same route to get to it every single day. He has no real hobbies outside of work (you'd be surprised how often I hear people say this), and likes to watch the same TV programs every night. Sunday always involves a sleep-in, and then his favourite afternoon sport on TV.

~ **Imogen:** by contrast, Imogen's had a few different jobs – some of them overseas. She takes six weeks holiday every year, going to a new location each time. She's constantly taking her family out to see and do new things each weekend. She's a voracious reader, into CrossFit and yoga, and likes to try out a new hobby or challenge each year. This year, she's learning Salsa.

DON'T
ignore all the
inspiration around
you.

Who do you imagine has a better mindset for fresh ideas: Robert or Imogen?

If you said "Imogen", you'd be right. She has a lot more variety in her life than Robert. As such, she has much more material to draw on when fresh thinking is required. You need a dynamic person like Imogen at the heart of your organisation's culture of innovation.

Of course, that doesn't mean Robert isn't a great person, or that he doesn't do an amazing job. Rob is a reliable legend around the office. It also doesn't mean that routines are bad things. Successful people often give strong routines credit for their ability to get shit done. But Imogen is the go-to person for ideas and inspiration. Robert can be too, of course – if he wants to be. He doesn't even need to make huge, sweeping changes to make that happen.

Let's say that Rob decides to change things up in his life a little. How might that look?

~ First, he starts reading different books, so he takes in more stimulation.

~ He opens his eyes and sees a whole bunch of unfinished jobs around his house. As he completes them, he develops his skills and brings some variety into his thinking.

~ He decides he'll go to the Saturday markets with his wife once a month, which gets him looking at things differently.

~ He decides to watch American Football one Sunday afternoon instead of his regular sport, and his thinking shifts.

~ He decides to catch the bus to work instead of driving, and listens to a podcast, which gives him a unique insight.

~ He gets to work, and a thought from the podcast keeps replaying in his head. He writes it down, musing, "Hey, I'd never thought of it like that." (Watch out, Rob: you just took your first step in developing an innovation mindset.)

~ He shares that idea with some teammates, and they discuss it excitedly. (Seriously, Rob, watch out: things are *really* happening now!)

Rob's lack of fresh thinking wasn't about a lack of time. It was about *how he spent the time he had.*

Everyone gets the same twenty-four hours in every day. We just all choose to spend it differently. There will always be travel to work, lunch time, coffee breaks, and having to wait for a meeting in another organisation's foyer. What could you do with all that time?

Each moment can be a mini-adventure for your mind if you just open your eyes. And opening them doesn't take any extra time: it just takes a slightly different approach.

My art school lecturer once gave me a tip to change my perspective that *literally* takes only a second. When you're looking at a painting, he told me, try squinting. When you squint, it blocks out the distracting details, leaving only the strong colours. That way, you can easily see which blocks of colours work in your painting, and which you might need to change. It allows you to see in a new way.

That one tiny shift enabled me to see all my artworks with a completely different mindset.

The great book *Become an Explorer of the World* by Keri Smith takes this idea into our everyday lives. She encourages us to truly take notice of what we see around us, exploring and documenting it to drive our creativity and imagination. Some of her points on how to be an explorer of the world are:

~ Always be looking.

~ Everything is interesting. Look closer.

~ Notice the stories going on around you.

~ Notice patterns and make connections.

~ Use all of your senses in your investigations.

This approach could also be called *An Innovator's Manual*. What Smith suggests doesn't take any extra time. It just requires you to be open to what's already around you, and always keep looking.

Artist Grayson Perry said, "It's an artist's job to notice things that other people miss". You can easily replace the word "artist" there with "innovator".

Inspiration can literally come from anywhere if we look for it. Innovators see things that other people miss because they observe life with open eyes. They see information and patterns that others overlook. They make connections that other people miss. They're always looking at the world around them.

Remember that trip?

Think of an overseas trip you once took that you really enjoyed. If you have kids, take it a step further back and remember a trip before they were born (back when you had plenty of free time). The "free time" is important here, incidentally, so don't choose your three-week Kontiki trip around Europe. Seeing the inside of night clubs and then sleeping all day doesn't really work for this example.

For any other trip, though, I want you to imagine yourself back there now. Imagine how, from the moment you get to the airport, things are different. You notice a different feel in the air, which even smells different.

On the way to your accommodation, you notice all the different neighbourhoods that you drive through. Cars and buses all look different. You check into your hotel, then go for a wander in the streets.

As you walk, you look at everything with wide open eyes. You're noticing details: the tablecloths at the cafe you walk past; and the way the chairs are slightly different to the ones at your local at home. Even the cobblestones on the street are unique.

You tune in to the different dialects you're hearing. People are wearing different clothes. Your eyes pull apart all the things you can see in the shop windows. You hear music that's the complete opposite of what you'd normally listen to. There's a window frame that looks so amazing with the way the light hits its flaking paint that you just have to stop and take a photo.

Then, when you sit down for a meal, wishing you'd worked harder on learning the language, you notice the feel of the menu in your hands.

At least you've learnt one phrase, though; "Dos cervezas, por favor," (or its local equivalent), which you know gets you two beers. But even then, you can't help noticing that those beers arrive in long, thin glasses that are so different to home.

I could go on, but you know what I'm saying, right? When we travel, we notice everything. We make the effort to notice, deliberately opening our eyes to everything around us. (That's why, when we come back from overseas trips and experiences of a new culture, our brains are generally in overdrive.)

Do you ever open your eyes like this at home? Think of the last time you walked in to work from your car (or however you commute). Generally, you keep your head down, checking your phone for messages, moving fast, and noticing only enough to dodge other people's feet.

It's ironic that so many people travel to the other side of the world to see things that they regularly ignore at home.

What great things could you have missed in just that small walk to your office from your car, bus, or train? What great ideas might have sparked if you'd just opened your eyes a little more, and looked up instead of down. No matter how busy you are, glancing up from your phone doesn't take any more time (or even any more effort.)

I once spent six months in the United States when I was younger (I've always been a huge traveller). When I got back, I realised that I knew New York City much better than I knew Sydney, my home city. I'd explored New York with a different set of eyes to the ones I looked with at home.

So, once I was home, I put on my "traveller's hat" and explored Sydney with a fresh set of eyes. Because I was at university and had MUCH more spare time, I discovered that there were so many interesting things to see locally when I looked for them.

Looking at life with "traveller's eyes" will generate fresh thinking in any space, work or otherwise. It will form new connections. You'll get clues and insights from shop windows, or from whatever people are wearing and saying. Clouds in the sky that look like a donkey riding a giraffe will become a total thought shifter.

Don't ignore all the inspiration around you.

Exercise: Shoot it

Photography is a great way to record the world around you. It helps you to look at your surroundings in a unique way. You're literally seeing things through a different lens: one that helps you to see detail and opportunities that others can easily miss.

So grab your phone and start photographing. Take at least one photo per day for the next four weeks. There's great photo material everywhere, and looking for it will force you to see it.

You could even make this a team-wide challenge. Get everyone in your team to take one photo per day, and share the photos with each other the next day.

If you need ideas to get you started, here are a few:

- *Shadow*
- *Ripples*
- *Coffee*
- *Texture*
- *Energy*

Share your photos, print them, and get busy. A whole world of stimulation and fresh insight is waiting.

At the end of this book, you'll find instructions to download your free photography guide, along with plenty of ideas to inspire you to look through the "different lens" of photography.

Changing the way you look at the world around you is easy, quick, and creates a non-stop idea-stimulation funnel. Whether you're at work or not, ideas are everywhere. If you let them in, great things will come out.

Another easy way to stimulate ideas is to keep your environment fresh. And that's what the next section's all about.

Change your physical environment

Imagine this strategic thinking scenario...

You're part of a leadership team that's on an offsite to do some deep, strategic thinking about the company's direction for the next four years. It's at a beautiful resort: a great place to unwind and relax your brain. You spend the first evening having drinks overlooking the beach, and the next morning having breakfast on the terrace overlooking a lake.

Your senses are on fire and you're feeling good.

Then, you and the team head to the training room for the first day. You go down a flight of stairs into a dim, beige room with no natural lighting, that's set up in typical boardroom style. There's a flipchart with a red and green pen, a jug of water in the corner, and a bowl of Mentos on the table. Someone draws the curtains to kill the tiny sliver of natural light that just peeked in… and your day is ready to start.

Welcome to the most mind-numbingly boring *place in the world.*

Welcome to the inspiration-killer, the imagination-choker, and the innovation-squasher. Rooms like this are an inspiration desert… yet, for most companies, this is simply Strategy Day reality.

Combine this environment with sitting for far too long, and eating far too many Mentos to relieve the boredom… and you have a recipe for fresh thinking disaster.

The term "offsite" has unofficially come to mean "an onsite somewhere else". What *should* be a fresh change becomes just a normal day elsewhere. You still have the same pressures, the same physical environment (or worse), and the same number of phone calls.

It's no surprise that this type of environment produces *exactly* the same BAU thinking you had at work. (And remember: innovative cultures can't thrive with this thinking.)

Your physical environment has a HUGE impact on the quality of your ideas. Just as your thought patterns change when you're on holiday, your daily physical environment massively alters the quality of how you think.

New environments trigger new ideas. Stimulating your senses makes new connections, which then creates new labels and files in your brain.

How conducive is your working environment to great ideas?

Is it time to refresh your workspace? The right environment is imperative if you want to produce quality creative results.

I've walked into many offices over the last fifteen years. And I can usually tell a lot about the company culture by the energy I feel and the way the office is laid out.

Compare these two examples…

Office 1: *Everything's silent. I'm not sure where the interior designer got their inspiration or their degree from, but they seem to have aimed for communist-era chic. The drab, grey walls, cubicles, flickering overhead lights, and furniture inevitably go hand-in-hand with low, low energy and a generally crappy vibe. Who wants to work in a space that looks like a KGB office in a James Bond movie?*

Those grey offices can be soul-destroying.

Office 2: *The first thing I notice are the different colours on the walls – not a single grey cubicle in sight. Natural light streams in, and there's a nice mix of workspaces. I see different textures and surfaces, with plants by the desks, and interesting things on the walls. Most importantly, there's variety.*

In this office, there's a pulse.

How to change your environment

So, what do you do if you find yourself in an office with Soviet-era design themes? Or if your facilities manager (a 6' 8" ex-cage fighter with no sense of humour) has pinned a very strong, passive-aggressive message on the noticeboard about the consequences of changing anything.

Here are four easy things you can implement straight away.

1. Start by adding some colour to your general workspace

The world is so much more interesting with colour. Assuming that you don't want to risk your facilities manager's wrath by painting a wall, some easy options are:

~   A bright chair

~   An outlandishly coloured kettle in the kitchen

~   Some amazing coasters for your mugs or glasses

~   Your Nan's crocheted blankie over the back of your office chair

2. Put interesting things on your walls or desk – and encourage your team to do the same

This is closely related to Point 1, but at a more individual level. The things you use don't have to be expensive – just go for anything that catches your eye.

You can easily get your hands on posters of some great artworks. I'm also a huge fan of repurposing other things to create art for a wall. Maybe try:

~ Typography

~ Illustrations

~ A poster for an exhibition

~ A vintage advertisement

If none of those appeal, pick up any home decorating or design magazine (well… maybe not *A Country Manor*, with a stuffed fox above the mantle) to give you great options you can tear out and frame.

3. Create a mood board and/or an idea capture space

Place a whiteboard or chalkboard in your office, or somewhere you'll walk past every day, that you can easily write or draw on. Not only will it give you a great way to record your ideas, but it will also add variety, stimulation, and freshness.

4. Add some plants

Plants are awesome. They not only do great things for the air that you breathe, but they're also known to boost productivity, happiness, and wellbeing. Given the amount of time we all spend in urban environments, it's imperative to bring a little bit of nature close to us.

Other ideas to keep your environment fresh

~ Try to work offsite at least once each week. If you have a task that lends itself particularly well to a coffee shop, go and do it there.

~ Schedule a one-to-one with a teammate in an outdoor space.

~ Take a client to an art gallery cafe in your city for a meeting. Tell them your story of wanting to change your environment to shift thinking.

~ Meet with people while walking. Bill Clinton was a fan of the walking meeting during his presidency; and Aristotle was also said to walk as he taught.

~ Hold your next offsite somewhere a little more edgy. Awesome spaces are opening everywhere, including art galleries, dance studios, acting schools, and reclaimed waterfront warehouses. Any of these options will help to turbocharge your mind.

~ Use brightly coloured Post-it notes to record any inspiration you have at your desk.

~ Whatever you do, have fun!

The key takeaway here is that *every* office needs some variety and stimulation. It's not only great for productivity and creativity, but for happiness as well.

Dr. Craig Knight, along with a team from Exeter University and four other global universities, led a study into the effects of a lean (spartan) office environment. He summed up the results of the study succinctly as, "If you put an ant into a 'lean' jam jar, or a gorilla in a zoo into a 'lean' cage – they're miserable beasties." He then added that, "People in lean offices are no different."

The way that you design your space says a lot about who *you* are as a person as well. Think of the impression that you want your team to have when they come into your workspace. Do you want them to leave thinking they've just spent a winter in Siberia OR just gone for a skateboard in Innovation Town?

Wear your "Grand Designs" hat

Of course, you won't be able to completely redesign your office, but take a walk around it, and look for all the creative dead spots. These are areas that send a small "lack of inspiration" shiver up your spine.

(Note: if you're in the cleaning closet when you feel this, move elsewhere. This space is not your fight.)

Make a note of each space, and then write list of all the things that you can do to brighten them up that won't break the bank.

You could even hold a challenge, and encourage your team members to do the same with their individual workspaces to create an overall environment that provides more inspiration.

Take the steps you need to brighten things up, and create a great space for thinking and action. Send a message to your brain that you're in an innovative environment. At the same time, send a message to your team that *they're* in a creative space where great things happen.

And once you've done that, it's time to consider exactly *how* you're going to work with your team, too.

Should you work collaboratively or solo for great ideas?

There's a constant debate raging over whether the best creative thinking and ideas come from working by yourself or collaborating with a group. And depending on whether you label yourself an introvert, an extrovert, a yellow/blue/green mix or an Eagle/Golden Retriever cross (or whichever animal label your personality test spits out), you'll get a different answer about what works best.

My thoughts? Working collaboratively and working solo can both be great for developing outstanding ideas. Each person is unique; and different things work for different people at different times. Great ideas can come in those serene moments when we're alone and taking a break from daily routine. They can also happen when people bounce ideas off each other.

Everyone's unique, so what works for you won't necessarily work for your team. Just remember that you'll need to be open to both options to identify what works best for everyone involved.

I get great benefits from thinking by myself, but I love the energy and idea-building that happens when my team are all together too. I also love the collaboration that comes when people connect with the unique skills, diversity, and backgrounds of others.

I don't know who originally said, "Collaboration is not about gluing together existing egos. It's about the ideas that never existed until after everyone enters the room." Whoever it was, though, they got the point across beautifully. Working collaboratively can take thinking and ideas to a place that may not have existed beforehand.

In the words of George Bernard Shaw, "If you have an apple and I have an apple and we exchange these apples, then you and I will still each have one apple. But if you have an idea and I have an idea and we exchange these ideas, then each of us will have two ideas."

Does everyone have to agree?

Hell, no! It can be hard for people to get their heads around the concept, but not everyone has to have the same viewpoint. We all have our personal way of thinking, which can be both a blessing and a curse. It's a blessing in that it gives us unique insight and perspectives. But it's also a curse, in that we can think our insight and perspective is the only possible right view.

In a culture of innovation, opposing viewpoints are valuable – and valued. Different viewpoints bring insight, new perspectives, and freshness of thought. Tensions are fine. Ideas butting up against each other are great.

In fact, it's often the interplay in those tensions that creates diverse new connections and patterns of thought. Whilst "a clash of ideas" may sound like the latest instalment in the *Game of Thrones* saga, it's actually a good thing. The last thing you want as you explore ideas is "groupthink", where everyone agrees with the loudest voices in the group because they're scared to speak up, don't want to upset anyone, or just know no other way.

It should be *impossible* for a diverse, creative team to all have the same viewpoint. They may share common principles and values, but the richness of an innovative team lies in the differing perspectives that come from their unique backgrounds and experiences. A great culture of innovation can only exist when it's OK to have opposing ideas. And great ideas can only happen when group members argue their individual viewpoints and then build on each others' contributions.

The "Innovation Sweet Spot" exists between two – or more – wildly opposed views.

"For good ideas and true innovation, you need human interaction, conflict, argument, debate."
– Margaret Heffernan TED speaker and Author

How to collaborate successfully

The first rule of collaborating well is to simply not be an arsehole. Put your ego aside, and accept that you're probably not the smartest person in the room. It doesn't *have* to be your way or the highway. That should solve most of your problems before they even begin.

As for the rest? Here's a quick guide to what to do, what not to do, and why.

First, let's look at what you DON'T want to unfold

Imagine that someone – let's call him Jonesy – presents an idea at your team meeting. Immediately, as is typical, other attendees begin to tear the idea down. As we've talked about before, it's much easier for most people to see what's crap about an idea before they see what's great about it.

Jonesy naturally gets defensive, at which point there's plenty of laughter and mocking. The idea-reviewers all have their blinkers (remember meeting those in Chapter 4?) on. "Ahh, Jonesy," they chortle. "You always say the most ridiculous things, mate." Everyone leaves that meeting feeling worse than when they walked into it (and vowing never to offer *their* ideas for fear of the same treatment).

So not only is Jonesy's idea well and truly dead, but it's the last time anyone in the team will stick their neck out. Talk about an innovation killer.

Here's a FAR better collaboration scenario

Great collaboration can benefit from structure. What would happen if the team followed a process a little closer to the one below?

Step 1 – What's great: this time around, Jonesy presents his idea for solving a problem to the team, who've all agreed to maintain a mindset of "let's build on this and grow something great".

Each team member has different thoughts on Jonesy's idea, but instead of immediately zeroing in on what they don't like, they take the opposite approach. They each think through what they like about the idea, and how it could help with the problem they're trying to solve.

Each person writes down their own thoughts, and then shares them with the room.

Step 2 – What could be improved: next, team members each list all the things they think could improve the idea. What needs adding to it to solve this specific problem? They each give reasons for their opinion, and explain how their experience and background contributed to it.

Then the team explores everything that needs to be reviewed with the idea. What still isn't clear? What concepts are they still struggling with?

Step 3 – Learnings: after this, team members explore what their individual and group learning and a-ha moments were. They create action points, and make a note of who'll do what, by when.

Step 4 – Repeat: Jonesy's idea is now alive, moving, and so much stronger than before, because it's been built upon by all the great minds in the room. The diversity of thinking that went into the now-evolved idea will make it a far stronger solution.

Beware: group discussions often end up controlled by one or two people, which is where groupthink can happen. This is why some experts believe it's better to come up with ideas by yourself.

When this happens, it moves the conversation from collaboration to domination, which takes the fun out of what you're doing. Not only that, but it invites everyone's Ogres back into the room. If you see this happening in your meeting, call these fools out and tell them to take a chill pill. (And make sure you're not doing it yourself either.)

This type of chest-beating behaviour just doesn't belong in a culture of innovation.

> *"I always find that if two (or more) of us throw ideas backwards and forwards, I get to more interesting and original places than I could have ever have gotten to on my own. But there is a danger, a real danger, if there's one person around you who makes you feel defensive, you lose the confidence to play, and it's goodbye creativity".* – John Cleese.

Give it a go in real time

1. *Next time you have a specific problem to solve, present it to your team with the instructions to build on each others' ideas, rather than tearing them down. Get them to first talk about what they like about each idea that's generated, and how it would help to solve the problem.*

2. *Next, each team member needs to make a list of all the things that would improve on each idea, along with their reasons, and how they've come to that conclusion. Then move the discussion to what might not be clear, or what they're struggling with conceptually.*

3. *Ask each team member to share their fresh insights and a-ha moments, and discuss them.*

4. *Get into action! Make a list of the action steps that will have the most impact in solving your problem, then set due dates for each step, as well as who will do what, by when.*

5. *Repeat. Continue to build on the ideas and diverse opinions for each new problem you have. Keep generating new ways to look at solutions for old problems.*

For me, it comes down to remembering that great ideas develop in different ways for different people. That will never change. However, even given that, the ability to collaborate on ideas and build on others' thinking still lies at the heart of a culture of innovation.

No matter how good we think we are, no one ever created an empire by themselves.

The over-analytical death roll

Before I move on to talking about the levers you can pull to kick-start the flow of ideas, let me introduce you to something I call "the over-analytical death roll". This is an all-too common phenomenon in the corporate landscape that can spike great ideas and innovation straight in the eye, so you *need* to be on the watch for it.

You've probably seen the over-analytical death roll take place many times, especially at office meetings and conferences. And due to its ability to travel, it even follows people around from place to place, making regular appearances each year.

Here's why the over-analytical death roll is so common

Our brains love to take the path of least resistance. They go straight to the easiest, most accessible files – usually the ones they created earlier. And sometimes, as we discussed in Chapter 4, that can be an efficient way to do things.

But in a large organisation, the path of least resistance with a new idea is often endless analysing, talking, analysing, talking, analysing, and – you guessed it – more talking. Three hours later, nothing more has happened, and nobody's getting anywhere.

Why do I call it a death roll?

Picture this: a group of really switched on people get together to talk, plan, strategise, and explore. A small piece of fresh thinking – a tiny shred of potential innovation – comes out.

That's when it starts. Everyone starts listing all the overly analytical reasons that the idea won't work. It's like some kind of large, urban crocodile sways into the room and wraps itself around everyone. Once it has the team tightly enclosed, its death roll starts.

The conversation starts going deeper and narrower, instead of wider to get more fresh insight. The death roll goes on and on, crushing any further fresh thinking into oblivion. It just doesn't stop.

One brave team member tries to jump in with an original idea… but six hands rise, giving a, "Don't talk, we're still analysing the last idea!" vibe. And the death roll continues. The person who originally had the great idea generally gives up at this point, knowing it's easier to just stay quiet, lie back, and go with the death roll.

This swarming, crocodile-wrapped mass of analysis is so powerful that if you tried to stop it by poking a stick into the middle of it, that stick would snap, disappear, and be consumed. If you were wandering past, you'd probably be sucked in. What started off as seven people can end up as nine or ten, including the cleaner and a maintenance manager who couldn't make it past the door.

Finally, the death roll stops when lunch is announced. There are loads of sighs, heavy faces, and a general lack of energy in the room. There's nothing fresh or new – just lots of analysis and back-and-forth conversation about the same thing. (And perhaps a very satisfied looking crocodile.)

Look, I haven't made this up. The people I work with tell me, "Simon, we're lawyers, accountants, or salespeople. We're great at analytical thinking, but crap at anything else". It's paralysis by analysis.

Analytical thinking is great when it's needed. It's *essential* for certain stages of innovation. There's no use in having ideas if you don't know the problems they're solving. And you need analytical thinking to test the ideas further down the track. At this stage of innovation, however, you need a different kind of thinking.

Albert Einstein mused that problems are rarely solved within the same mindset that created them. In other words, if you want to solve a problem, you need to shift your thinking.

Going wide in your thinking

To solve a problem, you need to go very wide in your thinking. Going wide is at the opposite end of the spectrum to the over-analytical death roll, and it needs to be a conscious decision. You need to develop the ability to recognise when your thinking is narrow, and then take it wide.

Making this choice is about changing your brain's default setting for deep, narrow thinking. It's about ensuring that you don't go straight to the same file you'd usually head to when you respond to a new idea.

Think of it as like being at a Wet'n'Wild waterslide park. You climb a very long ladder, and you're at the launch zone. From this point, there are four different slides that you can go down. You like the red one – you've always taken red – and that's been great in the past. But red will always end up in the same place. You'll have fun, but it will be the same fun every time.

Choosing one of the other slides gives you a different experience, and you don't know what it will be like. You know there'll be many twists and turns along the way, but they'll be *different* twists and turns. Choosing to take a different ride will give you more options to enjoy, instead of going for safe old red all the time.

I'm going to repeat this point because it's important: going wide is a choice. Staying narrow is a bad habit that you need to break (albeit one we're all guilty of). And the early stage of the innovation process is when you need to take your thinking *very* wide. As you work your way through the innovation funnel (just like that ping pong ball on crack), your thinking can start to narrow. For now though, you need all the options that wide open thinking brings with it.

For many organisations, the over-analytical death roll has become BAU thinking. You and your team need to start recognising the death roll, and using some death roll breakers when you see it. You need to loosen the crocodile's grip.

And that's what the next part of this chapter will help you to do.

(OK: time for that coffee break now – or a herbal tea if you're on a detox. Take your time – I'll be waiting once you've had your hot brew.)

PART 2 – POST CAFFEINE BREAK

Creative levers to pull

Let's stop talking about "creative thinking tools"

I must be honest: I'm *not* a fan of the terms "creative thinking tool" or "creative technique". In fact, I really struggle with the concepts, because a tool by itself is worthless. It's just a tool.

Talking about "creative thinking tools" is like going over to someone who's looking at a broken-down truck, giving them a shifting spanner, and saying, "Go for it". Sure, they now have a tool. But unless they also have some understanding of engines, the right mindset and enthusiasm, some context, and an idea of where to *use* that tool, the spanner by itself is just a piece of metal.

A tool can be useful; but on its own, it's not the answer.

I've experimented with a lot of approaches over the last ten years, believing that because a structured thinking tool was the standard consulting industry way to go, it was somehow necessary. But I found that, much like the spanner, thinking tools by themselves were useless.

Perhaps I should have trusted the instincts I developed as an art student at university. We were never schooled in standalone creative thinking tools or techniques that we had to follow line by line. Instead, we were introduced to ideas, given briefs, and shown techniques of how to do or create "X". Then we were simply told to get off our arses, build, experiment, prototype, and make it happen.

Through this process, we developed amazing creative skills, and a brilliant way of looking at the world. The process of exploration, experimentation, and prototyping lit an innovation fire in our imaginations.

With that in mind, I'm not going to talk about "creative tools" in the next few sections. I'm going to reframe the concept of "tool" to "lever". I'm going to introduce you to different levers that you can pull up or down to shift the way that you think.

But... be aware that like tools, these levers aren't the answer in isolation. Using Lever X doesn't guarantee 100% success each time. Instead, it simply offers you a fresh perspective – the type you need in a culture of innovation. Sometimes that lever may work exactly as you thought it would. Sometimes it won't. You'll usually need to pull more than one lever at a time too: in my experience, the answer usually comes from pooling different resources together.

As a culture of innovation takes hold, you'll find yourself subconsciously pulling different levers all the time; which will naturally keep your imagination alive and your thinking fresh. Those levers will then become part of your collection of resources for solving your greatest challenges and getting your innovation mojo happening.

Plus, the levers I introduce are a great way to take the thinking in a traditional meeting (which is where it's most often needed) to another level. They force your brain to make new connections, rather than relying on a BAU approach. Remember: your brain loves the path of least resistance. Creative levers can help to stop your brain from following that path, and change the way you think and behave. That in turn will create a different result.

WARNING: don't expect a single morning of brainstorming using one creative lever to create the innovation you want. Creative thinking is only a *small* part of the story. The rest is about getting off your backside and repeatedly practising behaviours that get your company moving towards a culture of innovation.

Have some fun, play around, and experiment. A thousand little lightbulb moments await.

Outrageous Disruption

I'm going to start with one of my favourite levers to pull: Outrageous Disruption. I've found that almost everyone can connect with this idea – perhaps because the word "disruption" is everywhere in the corporate space. So being allowed to have a disruptive mindset really enables people to shift their thinking.

Here are the questions to ask to pull this lever:

~ What would the ultimate disruption be in your industry?

~ If you could do something outrageous to meet your clients' needs and solve their problem what would it be?

~ What would turn your industry on its head?

Of course, there's plenty of discussion around what true disruption is and isn't – who's doing it and who's only improving a process. For the sake of taking your mind for a wander, though, try working with these examples.

~ **Airbnb:** What if we made an accommodation network where we didn't supply any accommodation? What if customers had thousands of options beyond hotels? Hello travel industry shakeup.

~ **Netflix:** What if we created content that our customers could access 24/7 on demand? Bye bye video store and late fees.

~ **Sanitarium Health Foods:** What if breakfast cereal was something that came in a handy drink for time-poor customers? Hello Up and Go.

INNOVATION
is a *people* thing, not a process thing.

~ **New York City pastry chef Dominique Ansel:** What if we combined two great tastes – a croissant and a donut – and made a cronut? Hello heart attack, and hello disruption.

~ **Salesforce:** Why does it has to be so hard to buy and use enterprise software? Hello success.

~ **Apple:** What if a phone was also a personal computer in your palm? Hello new normal.

~ **Uber:** What if a taxi could turn up wherever you wanted it, instead of you having to look for a taxi rank? What if we created a taxi network where we didn't own or supply any of the taxis? Goodbye frustrated customers.

Of course, you may not be looking for complete industry disruption – and if not, don't stress. This creative lever also drives brand new perspectives, which (as we've mentioned before) is a very good thing. As the classic saying goes, rules – and paradigms – are made to be broken. Outrageous Disruption is a great way to bust out of some of those paradigms. It's permission to go wild in your head and simply disrupt.

Let's use breakfast cereal – a product that's seen plenty of changes over the last few years – as an example. Take your mind back twenty years, and check in with the assumptions that you had around cereal back then:

Assumption	Disruption
Eaten in a bowl with a spoon	Eaten in a bar or as a drink
Eaten at the breakfast table	Eaten on the go
Healthy	Eaten as a dessert or treat (chocolate in muesli)
Must pour milk on it	Comes ready to eat with yoghurt or fruit on top

Remember: pulling a creative lever to shift your thinking probably won't give you the immediate solution that you need. (Of course, breaking that immediate "We have an answer. Move on." paradigm is disruption in itself.)

What the Outrageous Disruption lever provides is insight and a new perspective. It's a great way to take your thinking very wide, which – as we mentioned earlier in the chapter – gives you far more options to consider. There'll be plenty of time to narrow down later.

Let's get disruptive

1. Ask: What's our problem? Where are we stuck?

2. Ask: Exactly who is our customer? Who are we trying to solve this for?

3. Create a page with two columns.

4. On the left, write down everything you think of as absolute truths, assumptions, or industry clichés associated with your problem. These were most likely true once (thus still hanging around), but may no longer be relevant or impactful. List as many as possible.

5. On the opposite side of the page, write down as many absolute disruptions to that rule as possible.

Don't get caught in all the reasons why a given disruption won't work. The aim is to leave pre-conceived ideas behind, and come up with as many possibilities as you can.

Remember: a culture of innovation comes from taking your thinking wide whenever you need to, and harvesting the amazing ideas that come from that.

Steal, poach and borrow

"Steal", "appropriate", "pilfer", "acquire", and "swipe": they all sound so dishonest, don't they? I promise, though, they're not.

Innovation involves connecting things that others miss – usually things that already exist. All ideas involve combining other ideas. Austin Kleon, author of *Steal Like an Artist* says, "Nothing is original, so embrace influence, collect ideas, and remix and re-imagine to discover your own path".

How do you do this? It happens through reading, looking, connecting, or simply being alive and being prepared to look a little further. Really, it's about going a little extra distance to get some great insight.

Realise, though, that stealing, poaching, and borrowing all create a slow drip-feed of inspiration. In a world that demands immediate results, this technique can move a little slower. However, it *will* give great results if you practice it regularly, which is why it needs to be front and centre in any culture of innovation. It's an important part of creating a culture that produces those thousand little lightbulb moments.

Below, I'm going to list some ways to approach this, so you can see how easy it can be.

Go external and ask questions

Look at what other companies are doing to solve similar challenges. There's *always* someone facing similar challenges. Always. They might not be in your industry, but that makes it even better.

For example, let's say you wanted to solve the following challenges. Here are just a few other companies you could look at, and questions you could ask…

~ **How do we get more people through our branches?**

Who else focuses on getting a huge amount of foot traffic, and has full stores of people?

- Smiggle?
- Service stations?

- Discount Stores?

- Top Shop?

- Supermarkets?

- Coffee Shops?

What are they doing that we can learn from?

~ **How do I ensure that people don't disturb our great culture?**

Which other companies have great cultures? What do they do to keep their culture sky high?

- Virgin?

- Atlassian?

- Salesforce?

What other 40-person startup could I check to see what they're doing?

~ **How do we articulate the value of services in a price-sensitive market?**

Who else charges a premium price for their product?

- Fashion Brands?

- Harrods Department stores?

- Penfolds Grange Hermitage Wine?

- Resorts?

How do they do that, and how can we?

~ **How do we create a tribe of people who are excited about our brand?**

Who else creates a fantastic tribe and has a great following?

- Famous presenters? Tony Robbins? Oprah Winfrey?

- Famous authors, podcasters, or bloggers? Tim Ferris? Seth Godin?

- Famous YouTubers? PewDiePie? Hola Soy German?

- Frequent flyer programs? Qantas? Virgin?

Who's doing this in the retail space?

- Dollar Shave club?

- VinoMofo?

What do they do that we don't?

~ **How do we waste less time on X?**

Who else needs to move at pace? What are they doing?

- Emergency services: Fire and Ambulance?

- Stock traders?

- News teams and reporters?

- Elon Musk and Space X?

How could what they do work for us?

Use internal company crowdsourcing for your idea

As you've seen, many people leave their creative selves (and all the associated knowledge) at home. This is a gold mine waiting for exploration.

Everyone in your organisation has had unique experiences in their lives. Careers twist and morph all the time, but the skills and mindsets of earlier jobs stay with us. That history is yet another gold mine.

I regularly run "Innovation Hackathons" with my clients. In these sessions, everyone in the team or organisation takes five to explore, create, and collaborate with their teammates. Team members have the time and space to draw on their past and present expertise and submit their best thinking for the most complex problems they need to solve.

Try running one of these at your next team meeting. (If you're not sure how, check out www.simonbanks.com.au for more details.)

Use external crowdsourcing for your idea

Unilever, a global leader in innovation, uses an open innovation portal to constantly seek new approaches and people to partner with to solve problems. Unilever says, "We want good technological ideas to become reality quickly for whoever thought of them first. We will consider partnerships with established suppliers, startups, academics, designers, individual inventors – anyone with a practical innovation that can help us meet our challenges."[1]

What I like about their approach is that they realise they don't have all the answers. They embrace diversity in both their own thinking, and who they're open to working with. They also recognise the importance of making things happen quickly. They know the market doesn't sit around for anyone.

Find a naive expert

Another approach is to find someone who knows absolutely *nothing* about your industry. Perhaps buy a friend a coffee (or something stronger), and take them through your problem. Their perspective will be completely different to yours; and my experience is that people generally love being asked for advice.

I mentor someone who's in a different industry to me, and when they tell me what they're going through, I come up with so many ideas to help them that it seems almost too easy. Changing my perspective and looking at someone else's problems also drives a completely new way of thinking for me.

A culture of innovation needs people with different perspectives. As the Victorian government says in its innovation statement, "Look for employees who understand your vision and align with your culture but aren't necessarily the same as you. Look for those that may have different perspectives, diverse backgrounds, passions, and capabilities."[2]

Start stealing

Take some time over the next few weeks to do the following:

- *Have a coffee with a friend who's in a completely different industry to yours. Run through some of the areas with them where you are stuck. I bet you get a few gems of insight.*

- *Take your team on an excursion. Think of another industry that's solving similar challenges to you. Go visit their stores, see their products, and meet their customers.*

- *Spend an hour doing some research on a company that you admire the hell out of. What are they doing that's working so well? Who can you take for lunch from that organisation to get some insight?*

At its most basic, stealing, poaching, and borrowing is nothing more than going a little extra distance to get some great insight. It's just research that's outside all the usual channels that your brain likes to go to first.

As the Indie Film maker Jim Jarmusch put it, "Nothing is original. Steal from anywhere that resonates with inspiration or fuels your imagination. Devour old films, new films, music, books, paintings, photographs, poems, dreams, random conversations, architecture, bridges, street signs, trees, clouds, bodies of water, light, and shadows. Select only things to steal from that speak directly to your soul. If you do this, your work (and theft) will be authentic. Authenticity is invaluable; originality is non-existent. And don't bother concealing your thievery – celebrate it if you feel like it. In any case, always remember what [French-Swiss film director] Jean-Luc Godard said: 'It's not where you take things from – it's where you take them to.'"

Someone else's shoes

There's a saying that to truly understand someone, you must first walk a mile in their shoes. If they're your enemy, this is great because you'll be a mile away, and they'll have no shoes. If they're not your enemy, however, you'll have some explaining to do.

Another way to see this scenario is that putting yourself in someone else's shoes is a great way to get fresh perspective. And if that seems a bit simple? Well, it is. But whilst it's very simple, it's not often practised.

Think of a recent story that drew a lot of media attention. It may have involved a new law passing, a prominent relationship breaking down or someone losing money. It's all too easy to loosely follow that story in the media and pass judgements like:

~   Hmmm, *I'd* never do it like that."

~   "How could that have happened?"

~   "I can't believe that. It's shocking."

~   "I'm outraged. What type of person would do that?"

As with many of these stories, however, once you understand the circumstances better, your thoughts completely change.

Now think of something that's happened in your personal life. It may have been an illness, an experience, or a situation that took real strength to get through. Whatever it was, it probably left you with an in-depth understanding and level of empathy for anyone else who experiences something similar. You're more driven to sympathise with and help others who've been through that same experience. Your thought patterns completely shift.

Until we experience the same things that other people do, we just don't have the same level of insight or empathy with their experience. And empathy *also* sits at the heart of user-centred design, which in turn sits at the heart of innovation.

> *"We spend a lot time designing the bridge, but not enough time thinking about the people who are crossing it."*
> *– Dr. Prabhjot Singh, Director of Systems Design at the Earth Institute*

I remember the first time I went across to an Apple Mac from a PC several years ago. When people asked what was it like, my reply was, "Apple has an icon to get you to where you need to go. A PC has a drop-down menu, and then more and more drop-down menus to get you where you need to go. Apple makes it really easy, while PCs seem to be designed for techies."

It's a basic explanation; but for me, Apple was easy to use and felt like it was made with my needs in mind.

Samsung then applied the same user-centred design process to smart phones by first making them much bigger, and then building on what customers felt was lacking in iPhones, i.e. a bigger screen.

Someone else's shoes

- *Write down what you're trying to achieve or the problem you're trying to solve. Also ask who you're solving it for.*

> - *Next, think of everyone who will interact with your issue. Cast your net very wide. Don't just think of the people who immediately interact with the problem: stretch and think of everyone, even at the problem's far edges.*
> - *Write down exactly what they're experiencing at every stage of problem.*
>   - *What are their needs?*
>   - *What are they thinking?*
>   - *What are they feeling?*
>   - *How are they behaving?*
>   - *How does it affect their environment?*
>   - *Will your current solution work for them?*
>   - *Will it solve their problems?*
>   - *Why or why not?*
> - *What insight does this give you that you didn't have before?*
> - *How will that affect the solution you're coming up with?*

Spending time in other people's shoes is important – even on the level of simple household items. Think about a household item you've bought that really pissed you off after you first used it. Now think of one that delights you. If you're anything like me, you sometimes use something and then wonder how the hell it was ever designed.

For example, we recently updated the toilet and bathroom in our house. Everything looks great, but the toilet seat is a real pain... in the arse (I had to say it). Due to a funky design quirk with the way the seat attaches, it constantly shifts around on the toilet. It's at a different angle all the time.

My kids hate using this seat: they go for a slide every time they sit down. We keep needing to adjust and tighten it... which is far too much time and energy to focus on a toilet seat. Whoever designed this seat had no empathy at all with their end users. Had they walked in someone else's shoes (or indeed, sat in their toilet seat)? I think not.

Think about online forms you've filled out that took 30 minutes to complete then crashed. Or a phone call about a problem that ended up bouncing you between fifteen departments over two hours (and still didn't end up solving the issue).

Think about trying to close or open a bank account, where you have to visit a branch during business hours.

Was there empathy for the user in the way that these processes were designed? If you have steam coming out of your ears as you think of your experience, then probably not.

Spending time in someone else's shoes is not only a great way to empathise with the people you're innovating for, and to get fresh perspectives. *It's also an invaluable human skill.* The Museum of Empathy, launched in 2015, is the first experiential arts space dedicated to helping people look at the world through other people's eyes. It aims to explore how empathy can tackle global challenges like conflict, inequality, and prejudice[3].

The museum's first exhibition, *A Mile in my Shoes*, required visitors to literally put on someone else's shoes and headphones. As people walked around the exhibition, they heard the story of the person being featured in the exhibition.

Remember: innovation is a *people* thing, not a process thing. It's what makes us human. People are at the heart of user-centred design, both as creators and users. So if you design to solve your customers' problems, it's happy days.

I was chatting with a team at a creative agency that I collaborate with. When I asked about their creative process and how they came up with ideas, they said they rarely struggled, because:

~   They collectively shared their ideas across the agency at the start of the project.

~ They made sure that everyone gave their perspective, regardless of their role in the brief.

~ In other words, they spent time in other people's shoes. This ensured they all had plenty of different insights, and that their idea funnel was full.

~ If one of the team got stuck at any time, they simply connected with other team members to share their thoughts, and the "stuckness" disappeared. Everyone was constantly walking in different sets of shoes.

The key thing I want you to understand is that there are great shoes to walk in everywhere. Each and every one of your customers has awesome shoes to walk in. The person who's been with your company the longest has a great set of experienced shoes. Your company's most recent hire has the most delightful, fresh, unique shoes to walk in. Their perspective is something that research can't easily buy, so get to them before they start thinking like everyone else.

Time to slip on some Crocs (but please, only for this exercise, and then never again), high heels, flip flops or Ugg boots.

There are great shoes to walk in everywhere. Get walking.

Embrace constraints

"CONSTRAINTS?!?", I hear you scream. "Constraints? There are no constraints in innovation. *All* crazy ideas are great. I'm on fire here – why bring out your fire hose and douse me with constraints? Are you trying to kill our creativity?"

Wait just a minute. Take a deep breath. I promise, it's just the opposite. It may sound counterintuitive, but there's method to my mayhem. Applying boundaries, parameters, and constraints to a problem forces a shift in your thinking and behaviour. As such, constraints can be another lever to pull when you're seeking a fresh perspective.

For example, a little while back, I was represented by an art gallery in Sydney. They had a sell-out sculpture show (a godsend for commercial galleries). And what made this exhibition different was its constraints:

~ Each artist had to use the same three pieces of metal.

~ The sculpture had to stand freely on the same-sized plinth.

~ All sculptures had the same price, regardless of the artist's experience or stature.

What each artist then did with the same pieces of metal was brilliant. Many years on, I can still picture the sculptures. The variety of the finished artworks was amazing. Rather than holding back the artists, the constraints forced them to make new connections, try new things, and experiment. The restrictions pushed their usual way of thinking and creating into a new space.

Today, I often get clients to design something visual, which requires them to draw. Initially, they just stare at a blank page, with no idea of where to start. Their hands hover just above the page – sometimes for five minutes or more. The initial blank canvas is just too much space; and instead of experiencing *paralysis by analysis*, they get *paralysis from too many possibilities*.

Then I jump in and make a few small marks on their pages. And suddenly (once they get over their initial shock and horror that I've ruined their drawing), they're up and away with their design. Why? Because they now have some constraints to work with. My few small marks give them building blocks and some boundaries. They can then build on what I've given then.

It's just the shift in perspective that they needed.

Add some constraints to shift your thinking

Write down your challenge, then apply some constraints to any solution.

See how it changes your thinking. Here are a few to get you started:

- *We need to do it in three days.*

- *We need to do it in one year.*

- *What could we do if we had no budget?*

- *What would we do if we had unlimited budget?*

- *What if we can't use email to communicate?*

- *What if we had no outside help?*

- *What if I had to do this by myself?*

- *What if our hands were tied behind our backs (literally)?*

- *What would I do if I could assemble any team I wanted for this?*

- *If we could only focus on one thing to solve this, what would it be?*

These constraints force you to shift your thinking, and provide fresh perspectives on the problem. Will these constraints provide an immediate answer? Possibly. Will they provide some new insights into the problem itself? Definitely.

Picture this

A client request comes in that needs to happen in two days. It's the sort of thing that would normally take ten days, but it must be done faster for some reason. Suddenly, your team jumps into action.

This time constraint unleashes a new style of thinking, behaviour, and attitude for them that's completely different to what would normally have happened. It creates new paradigms around what's possible.

Embracing constraints does more than just shift your thinking. Embracing real world constraints is actually vital to innovation.

So don't make constraints into a big whinge-fest about what you can't do. Allow them to help you unlock new ideas about what you could do instead.

The worlds of art, architecture, startups, sport, software, and design are all full of brilliant creators who embrace and adapt to their constraints. As the team from world-leading web development company Basecamp said in their book *Getting Real:* "Let limitations guide you to creative solutions. There's never enough to go around. Not enough time. Not enough money. Not enough people. That's a good thing.

When 37signals (the company's previous name) was building Basecamp, we had plenty of limitations… that forced us to come up with creative solutions. Constraints are often advantages in disguise. Instead, work with what you have."

Key things to realise

~ There will always be problems that need to be solved.

~ There will always be legacy issues beyond your control.

~ There will always be policies and procedures.

~ There will always be a budget that's lower than you wanted.

Embrace each of these constraints like a long-lost cousin. Don't let them become excuses – instead, turn them into the building blocks for innovative solutions.

~ If you use Twitter, you embrace the constraints of 140 characters.

~ If you use Instagram, you embrace that it's for photos and videos.

~ If your office Christmas party only has a budget of $1000, you embrace that and put on the best possible experience you can for your team for that price (and never really like your tight-arse boss again).

It's time to look at things differently. Constraints can be useful. Use them to shift your thinking and embrace them to power innovation, instead of believing that they hinder it.

99 Ideas

"Let's brainstorm this, people. Come on, give me your best ideas. Let's go." Cue the audience all rolling their eyes, and releasing a big sigh.

"Brainstorming" can be one of those words that make the good people in an organisation want to curl up and die inside. For many, it's as cringeworthy as blindfolded trust falls and hugging someone you don't know at a conference.

In short, brainstorming gets a *really* bad rap. Yet, amongst other people, it's the best tactic ever. Some people use it all the time. Others hate it with a passion. Done well, it can produce great results. Done poorly, which seems to be often, it can produce nothing more than a giant pile of crap.

Basically, there are a lot of mixed feelings, viewpoints, and even studies around how well brainstorming can work. So why all the variation? Think of brainstorming as being like a song – perhaps Adele's 2016 global smash hit *Hello*.

> **Scenario 1:** *Adele herself starts singing the song for you. Regardless of your taste in music, you're probably impressed with her voice. If she's the only person you ever hear singing it, you'd think this song was amazing.*

> **Scenario 2:** *Grandpa comes home from the bowls club, having beaten the visiting over-75s team from Silky Bay. After a few too many celebratory drinks with his team, he starts belting out the song.*

> *As the first mangled notes hit your eardrum, you think, "What the hell is that? Is that a donkey screaming?" If that's the only time you hear the song, you think it's terrible.*

Same song: very different outcome.

Personally, I hate the word "brainstorming" because of all its negative connotations. Alex Osborn, legendary advertising executive and the inventor of brainstorming, probably had no idea that his approach would be so contentious. He just thought that people working together would produce more ideas.

As I see it, the problem with brainstorming is not just that it's been done so poorly for many years. The problem is that it's been used in isolation, and seen as the ONLY way to generate fresh thinking. If you've got this far into the book, you know that creativity and innovation don't work like that.

There *is* no one perfect way.

My anecdotal evidence from watching or participating in brainstorming sessions is that people usually generate around 15–25 ideas before the stream dries up. At this point, everyone's expression starts shutting down, becoming something between bored and tired.

As we covered in Chapter 4, your brain loves the path of least resistance, so it goes to the easy places first. Plus, we're all striving for ultimate productivity, so we want to do things quickly and move on to the next task. What happens in practice is that those first 15–25 ideas generally come from that comfortable BAU thinking place. Then, once the easy ideas are down on paper, our natural reaction is to stop and go onto the next item on our to-do list. Get it done, smash it out, then go put out the next workplace fire. Busy, busy, busy!

Of course, that doesn't help us to come up with innovative ideas. Remember: the best ideas come once we're out of our comfort zones.

So although I *hate* the word "brainstorming", I *love* the "99 Ideas" lever, and the type of thinking it produces. The concept is that the freshest thinking usually comes from Ideas #70–#99. Great thinking happens at the edge of our stretch zones, not in the first few ideas where we're still firmly entrenched in our comfort zones.

THE
best ideas come once we're out of our comfort zones.

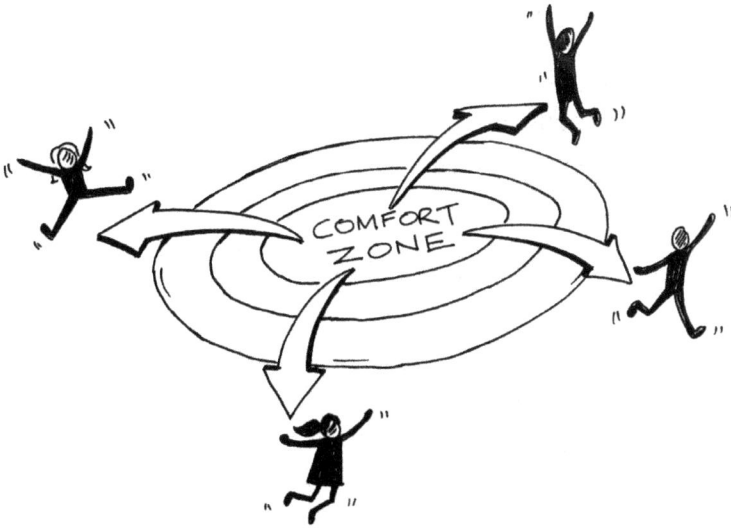

Here's a quick guide on how to use the 99 Ideas lever.

99 Ideas

Remove the word brainstorming completely from your language, and replace it with 99 Ideas. You're no longer going to brainstorm: you're going to generate 99 Ideas instead. Here are a few guidelines on how to do this well.

Firstly, get really clear on the problem you're trying to solve. *What do you need fresh insight on? Remember the ping pong ball on crack in a funnel? You can now start to work your way through your own innovation funnel.*

- **At the top of the funnel**, *go as far as you can with your thinking as you generate ideas. Let yourself get a little wild, and just aim for quantity. You want to end up with AT LEAST 99 Ideas (thus the name) as a minimum. If your group is bigger than six to seven, go higher.*

  Record your ideas in multiple ways. At the very least, write your thoughts in BIG letters on a Post-it note and stick it on a wall. Each person needs to explain their idea as it goes up. Use other people's ideas to stimulate your own thinking and ideas. Ask lots of questions. Keep your energy high. Turn off your Ogre. Oh – and of course, don't shoot down other people's ideas.

Remember: bad – or less than perfect – ideas are just part of the process. This is a big paradigm shift. As Seth Godin said when he was chatting with Tim Ferris, "The goal isn't to get good ideas. The goal is to get bad ideas. Once you have enough bad ideas, some of them will be a good idea."

At the next layer down, start to sift and group ideas.
Look for consistent themes and narratives. Can you naturally group these ideas together? What are the stories here? What jumps out at you? What are the connections?

Ask lots of questions like, "What are the best insights from these ideas?" and "What gaps are appearing?"

Keep building, not tearing down.

Then, at the next layer down after that: *apply your business filters to the ideas that have made it this far. What's feasible? What could happen quickly to create maximum impact? What needs more exploration?*

Keep asking lots of questions, and remember to keep the Ogre at bay. Now your initial 99 Ideas start to form some concrete insights...

Be prepared: *the 99 Ideas approach can be mentally exhausting. Get everyone standing or moving, and don't stop. Get some stimulation happening. Go for a walk, skip, or jump when your energy dips.*

Whatever happens, get to a minimum of 99 Ideas. The ideas towards the end may be some of the best. I like to add a short time frame to this process, but you can do this over a few hours or a few weeks. It's not time-dependent: the important thing is to just keep adding ideas.

Remember that brainstorming can be a problem when it's done poorly, or when it's the only way that teams seek fresh thinking. So go on, give the 99 Ideas lever a good shake. Spend some time in your stretch zone.

It's where a culture of innovation lives.

Walk, look and write

This approach is simple, and is one of my favourite ways to spark new ideas. It also recently led to a great creative success story for me.

I was invited to pitch for the design and delivery of a 200-person conference program. The potential client contacted me via email, giving me a two-line brief and contact details. After that, we kept constantly trying to catch up, with little success. This went on for a few weeks, meaning that getting any more information was difficult.

We eventually connected via email very late on a Thursday afternoon. The client gave me an indication of some of their conference themes, the WOW they wanted to see, and an indication of what they'd seen so far. Then they told me that my proposal had to be in by 11am the next morning to be presented to the leadership team. F.........antastic.

I started to think about what we could offer later that night, but I had *nothing*. It was late, after a week of very late nights and travel. My ideas vault was empty. Even my basketball game earlier that evening (which normally totally energises me) didn't help my brain come up with anything fresh. I had nothing other than a mood of mild panic.

So here's what I did:

~ I headed outside to change my environment.

~ I opened my eyes and took a thorough look around.

~ I took in some stimulation, and wrote down what occurred.

~ I waited to see what happened.

We live in a beachside town, so when I walk, I always have loads of eclectic gift shops, funky cafes, and other interesting things to look at. It was too late to head out at that point; so instead, I got up very early the next morning and started walking around all the shop windows in our town.

I took a very detailed look at *everything*, and wrote down all the interesting things I saw. When I truly looked, there was a huge amount of variety. Things that jumped out and caught my attention included colours, textures, photos, sculptures, quirky sayings, gift cards, and even great patterns on cushions and fabric.

As I continued to write down everything I saw, I felt a shift. Ideas started to bubble to the surface. I kept looking, writing more things down, and my thought patterns started to connect and build on each other.

I parked myself in a cafe about 45 minutes later with a huge list of words, ideas, themes, arrows, circles, and the odd drawing. I didn't have any of this the night before when I was stuck, but my mind (and notebook) was now crammed full. I went through the list and highlighted all the ideas that connected, took notes and went from there. Then, just over two hours later, I sent my proposal off.

The client absolutely loved my ideas, and we won the contract for the event. The conference activity we facilitated involved participants designing and theming a company-branded summer music festival that put the paying customer at the heart of the experience. (Oh, and the event went off brilliantly as well!)

Before I went through my "walking and looking" process, I had absolutely no idea of what form of event we'd propose. I certainly had no thought of a branded music festival: that was totally outside of our usual offerings. So what factors allowed me to generate that idea?

~ **Fresh air:** I was outside.

~ **Movement:** oxygen was pumping around my body as I walked. According to a recent Stanford Study[4], 60% of participants saw an increase in creativity when they were walking.

~ **Constraints:** the time constraints I was operating under created a sense of urgency and shifted my usual style of thinking.

~ **Changing my environment:** being in a new environment meant I saw – and was influenced by – different things.

~ **Conscious choice:** I made the conscious decision to truly open my eyes and be curious about everything I saw.

~ **Recording it:** I wrote down what I was seeing.

~ **Openness:** I was open to whatever I saw being part of the solution. I wrote down everything and just went with it. I didn't judge anything or cross it off my list.

Walk, look, write

Do I really need to explain this one?

Reread what I wrote above, then go and do it. This should be easy.

Oh – just make sure your pen works beforehand.

"Walk, look and write" combines several individual approaches for developing great ideas, and you can do it at any time. As with any habit, the more you practise it, the more natural and normal it becomes. Behaviour that's normalised within an organisation then becomes culture: in this case, a culture where market-leading thinking, great ideas, services, products, and results is just every-day normal.

An important part of creating an organisational culture of innovation at this stage is allowing yourself the time and space to go wide in your thinking and explore your idea. Hopefully, this chapter has given you a whole collection of ways to do this while you're generating problem-solving ideas that will delight your clients.

Framework #5:
Mock it up

When a sculptor is in the process of thinking, planning, and creating, they produce something called a "maquette". This is an old-school French word for a model or a smaller scale version of what they want to create. In other words, it's a rough draft.

Why would they produce something like this?

A maquette gives them a clearer idea of what their final product will look like before they actually create it. It gives them something tangible that all their senses can connect with. It lets them easily see what's working and what isn't, helping them to understand how that object may interact with its environment. It also provides powerful, instant feedback in a format that our brains like.

Physically mocking up a concept (aka "prototyping") is an essential and powerful part of innovation. And it's one that's sooooo often missed in the idea-development process.

Teams can put a huge effort into the ideation process, and produce nothing but a lot of written words. Unfortunately, words by themselves often lead to very one-dimensional thinking. The words move from flip chart paper to a report in a linear process with an end result that people can't easily interact with or explore.

A prototype, on the other hand, allows them to connect in a different way. It's interactive. Creating it and interacting with it involves movement and getting your hands busy. Because it engages several of your senses, it produces multiple viewpoints and perspectives. Most importantly, it takes something that's simply a concept and makes it *real*. Until a prototype is produced, an idea is just an idea.

The prototyping phase is essential because:

~ It's a safe place to make mistakes.

~ It's a great way to test your thinking.

~ It's a wonderful way to see if your idea actually addresses the problem you set out to solve.

~ It shifts your perspective, driving conversation and collaboration, and helping to open your thinking. It's like unpacking a suitcase to see what's inside.

~ It's a great way to get feedback from team members, customers, and clients who interact with your prototype.

~ It puts the end user at the heart of your problem

Physically producing a prototype, however, requires courage and bravery, because:

~ **The Ogre jumps in as soon as the initial prototype doesn't look perfect.** It's not meant to be perfect, of course, but Mr Ogre-Perfect-Pants sees this as an opportunity to throw some doubt your way.

~ **It can be fun.** It genuinely feels good to create and put things together. I've seen people get very worried when they have fun at work. They're not *supposed* to have fun at work. They're highly respected, very serious professionals, after all!

~ **The tools required to mock an idea up are very simple.** They look like the craft materials you probably had back at primary school. I've often run innovation sessions in rooms with colourful materials everywhere.

Someone senior who opted out inevitably drops their head back in and says something like, "Ohh, back to primary school, are we? Cute." Hello Ogre, and *thanks* hallway Ogre. Those comments annoy me – especially when one of the company values is supposed to be innovation.

However, if you can get past the doubts in your head, prototyping is where the magic happens. It's where things get real. Mocking something up is not only fun – it's highly valuable.

I recently worked with a design team at Questacon: The National Science and Technology Centre in Canberra. I fell in love the moment I entered that building. The foyer contained loads of tactile objects that I could put my hands on. There was a workshop on the floor with loads of machinery in it. It looked like a place where things happened.

On the floor where I worked, I saw piles of materials to mock things up everywhere. It was exactly like you'd find in a primary school: we had plenty of plastic pots, cardboard tubes and lids. There was even a sign that said, "Don't take, for experiments". They knew the importance of prototyping.

It's essential to remember that you don't need to aim for perfection with a prototype. The rougher and quicker you can create it, the better. This is exactly the right place to make mistakes and experiment – or, as we talked about in Chapter 7, to fail fast. You've only created a prototype, so there are no negative impacts. You just learn, and the mistakes you make here stop you making *much* bigger mistakes later on. They prevent you from wasting a whole lot of time, energy, human capital, and money.

How I learned the value of prototyping

In my first year of art school, I remember politely discussing the need to not produce a prototype for a bronze sculpture I wanted to create. The sculpture would be a flying horse that looked like it came from a cartoon rather than a nature magazine. I had sketches I was happy to work with; and obviously, I knew more than my lecturer.

Because this was a sculpture, however, he said that the drawings wouldn't be enough. With much indignation, I finally capitulated, and agreed that yes, fine, I'd create a maquette.

And what do you know, exactly as my lecturer had said, the physical prototype gave me some great insights. Large elements of my design weren't suited to bronze, and there were a number of structural issues that meant I had to completely rethink my design.

That was one of the many hundreds of a-ha moments I went on to have over the next four years. I ended up majoring in large-scale ceramic sculptures; and producing prototypes saved me not only weeks and months of time, but also gave me some of my greatest insight as well.

Buckminster Fuller, the American inventor and designer, said, "There is no such thing as a failed experiment, only experiments with unexpected outcomes."

So get busy. Ignore your Ogre when it tells you that adults don't make things. Prototype your ideas often and at speed. Keep your eyes open for insights and learning (and don't forget to smile).

A culture of innovation is not about sitting still – it's about getting your hands dirty.

How do you start to prototype?

Start by assembling the right materials. *Collect lots of multi-coloured cardboard, tape, pens, markers, string, sticky notes, wooden blocks, yoghurt containers, Lego blocks, glue sticks, and staplers to get you started. These are very basic materials that you can buy anywhere.*

Next, get very clear. *Ask, "What's the main problem we're addressing here?" Your prototype must convey that idea. Keep it as simple and clear as possible.*

Finally, just get started. *Prototyping is action-focussed, and doing anything is better than doing nothing. (As a bonus, it also helps you to avoid the over-analytical death roll.)*

- *If you're prototyping a process, draw a wireframe on a wall, then use sticky notes to mock it up.*

- *If it's something three-dimensional, build a model of it.*

- *You can also draw your prototype (more on that soon), which works for all formats.*

- *If your idea involves human interaction, prototype that interaction by acting it out. If your eyes are starting to roll at the idea of role playing, shame on you. Remember that innovation requires a different type of courage and bravery. It's not role play, it's real play.*

> ***Most importantly, seek insight from your prototype.***
>
> - *What do you see that you didn't previously?*
> - *What connections are you now making?*
> - *What is and isn't working?*
> - *Test it with your audience and get their feedback.*
> - *Test it with people who aren't your audience and get their feedback.*
> - *What can you refine, improve and make better?*

Google Adwords is a great example of what's possible through testing your idea, getting feedback, using that feedback, and constantly iterating and tinkering. Susan Wojcicki, Google's former Senior Vice President of Advertising and now CEO of Youtube, outlined this in an article about Google's Eight Pillars of Innovation[1].

> *"The best part of working on the Web? We get do-overs. Lots of them. The first version of AdWords, released in 1999, wasn't very successful – almost no one clicked on the ads. Not many people remember that because we kept iterating and eventually reached the model we have today.*
>
> *And we're still improving it; every year we run tens of thousands of Search and Ads quality experiments, and over the past year we've launched over a dozen new formats. Some products we update every day.*
>
> *Our iterative process often teaches us invaluable lessons. Watching users "in the wild" as they use our products is the best way to find out what works, then we can act on that feedback. It's much better to learn these things early and be able to respond than to go too far down the wrong path. Iterating has served us well. We weren't first to Search, but we were able to make progress in the market by working quickly, learning faster, and taking our next steps based on data."*

Here's the deal. Whether you're prototyping by making a 3D model, or you're drawing out a problem for a different view, you need to use something other than a linear, text-based approach to solving your problem.

By mocking up your ideas, you get to handle them and engage your sense of touch. This sparks different areas of your brain, which then creates far greater scope for finding solutions, as you have something physical you can comment on and interact with.

In short, prototyping makes your idea real.

A great way to do this quickly that you can do anywhere, anytime is to draw your idea. This then allows you to visualise it.

The power of visualisation

> *"Of all of our inventions for mass communication, pictures still speak the most universally understood language."*
> *– Walt Disney*

I'm a huge fan of visual communication as a means of exploring ideas, communicating, and prototyping. This approach has really gained traction globally over the last few years.

We're in the information age, and it's an exciting time. One of the problems, however, is that there's just so much information. We get bombarded by it, to the extent that our brain changes the way we take it in. We've now learnt to look at things and take in information far more visually. A 2011 study by Dr Martin Hilbert of the University of South California said that, as far back as 2007, we took in 174 newspapers (or 34GB) worth of data every day[2]. And that figure is only continuing to grow. The US Data Management Company Domo says that Americans now consume 18,264,840 MB (18,264 GB) of wireless data per minute[3].

That's why using pictures and words together is a winning combination. Think of what happens when you surf the internet: you linger on the websites that have great visuals. As for the text-heavy websites of only a few years ago? You just zoom past them – there's simply too much detail.

When you only communicate and explore ideas through text alone, you only engage part of your audience's brains. That means they won't remember the whole story.

A better way to remember stories

I once heard the brilliant indigenous speaker Jeremy Donovan talk about his life, and I was transfixed the whole time. One story that stood out involved him going to live with his grandparents in a small place called Shipton Flats at the feet of Cape York.

While he was there, his grandad took him to a place to teach him all the traditional stories of their people. Jeremy took his book with him to write everything down, but his grandad threw it in the fire, which really pissed Jeremy off.

When he demanded to know why, his grandad said, "Our stories have been told with pictures in the sand for thousands of years. If I draw them in the sand, you will remember then forever. If you write them down, you will put that book on a shelf, you will move house, and you will eventually lose the book and lose all the knowledge."

With that story forever locked in his memory, Jeremy continues to paint these images and dreamings as a way to remain connected to his ancestral country and teaching. He also uses the same principles of teaching to pass these stories to his own children and extended family.

The facts about visualisation are very clear: our brains love pictures more than they do words. Science clearly shows that for most of us[4]:

~   50% of our brains are involved in visual processing.

~   It only takes around 1/10 of a second for our brains to get a visual sense of a scene.

Think of processing information as being like putting together an IKEA furniture pack. There's you, an Allen key, a stack of pieces in various sizes, and some instructions. It's enough to ruin a Sunday afternoon at the best of times – but if you don't have pictures in the instructions, it gets around 300% harder.

Compare these two approaches to communicating information:

Option 1: Think of the last PowerPoint presentation you went to – one where the presenter used an old-school approach. They had boring, text-heavy slides that they just read out, sometimes with their back towards you. Can you remember the second line of text on the third slide from that presentation? I'm guessing not – it just doesn't happen.

Option 2: Now imagine that a keynote presenter had followed that speaker. She told stories, using slides that contained eye-catching, attention-grabbing pictures. Do you think you'd remember those pictures more easily than the text from the previous presentation? If you're like most people, the answer this time is "yes".

That's because most people's brains remember pictures more easily than they remember words. In fact, after three days, most people only remember around 10% of what they read, but up to 65% of the visual information they've taken in[5]. And chances are that you'll still remember the combination of pictures and stories years later too, because the pictures help your brain to remember the stories (and vice versa).

I remember another time when I was helping a global consulting/IT company to craft a compelling story for their major project pitches. I drew a picture for one team that summarised the problem they were trying to solve; and I can still remember their reaction when I presented it. It went a little like this: "That's #*$%#@ it! That's #*$%#@ it! We've been working on this #*$%#@ problem for six months, and you nailed it right there! Thank #*$%#@!"

I've always known that most people love visuals; but that was the point I realised that there was more to this drawing caper than just producing pretty pictures. It was a place of breakthroughs – for both me and the people watching the visuals.

The brilliant thing with drawing is that it quickly reframes the way we look at things. The Innovation Sweet Spot happens when multiple parts of our brains connect and interact. When I teach people to draw, they hit that Innovation Sweet Spot. They start to think both logically and creatively. It's a stretch that an innovation mindset needs.

The good news is that drawing is a learnt skill; and it's very easy for most people to build a decent level of competence quickly. If you're reading this, scoffing away and saying, "Nuh uh. It might be easy for others but you haven't seen ME try…" you need to check your Ogre. Go back to the early stages of the book for a refresh. Remember: the Ogre pops up whenever and wherever it can have the biggest impact. You need the same confidence and self belief to pick up a pen and draw as you do to develop a culture of innovation.

As we covered earlier, many people credit negative comments from their late primary/early high school art teachers as the reason they believe they're uncreative. So it's no surprise that the Ogre wants to jump in as you pick up your pen. It remembers the damage it caused last time, and can't wait to do more.

So tell the Ogre to go and hide in the toilet; and let's get started!

A quick introduction to drawing

Your initial aim with learning to draw is to get to the stage where you can visualise a simple flow diagram – one that consists of lines, shapes and patterns. Most people get to this point in around 30 minutes.

Then, at its most basic, all drawing is simply a combination of lines, shapes and patterns. In fact, to draw successfully, you really only need to master drawing lines and three to four shapes.

Let's start with lines

A line is simply what happens when you put the tip of your pen on the paper and move it from one point to another.

Take yourself right back to your first days in high school. If you're like many students, your first Year 7 art lesson was probably about lines. As an astute and eager student, you probably listened intently as your teacher said something like, "OK class, time to draw some lines. First, draw a *happy* line."

"Next, draw an *angry* line."

"Now a *crazy* line."

(And for grown ups, try drawing a *big-night-out-with-the-girls-from-work* line.)

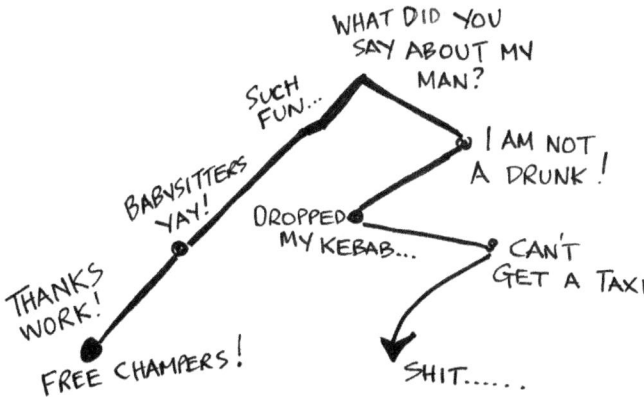

As you can see, simple lines can be highly expressive. And the great news is that *anyone* can draw a line.

Now let's move on to shapes

Shapes are what happens when you join a line back on itself. Simple!

The three most basic shapes that you need to draw are a circle/oval, a square/rectangle, and a triangle. With just these three shapes (or various squished versions of them), you can create almost anything.

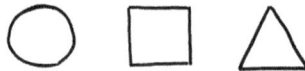

The fourth shape is an amorphous one that doesn't neatly fit into the other three. For example, try a cloud: it's a great way to show people thinking and group ideas, and it's very simple to draw.

Let's add patterns

Patterns happen the moment you repeat a shape or a line. For example, if you join circles together, you get a caterpillar.

At its heart, drawing is really about learning to see the shapes in things. Many people draw what they think they see, rather what they actually see. Artists plan their drawings out in shapes to get the proportions correct before they fill in the details around those shapes. Once they do, everyone goes, "Ohhh! Where did you learn to draw so well?"

The answer is that they did it by drawing the shapes.

Let's DRAW

Let's try this with something that's difficult. Grab a pen, and try combining shapes together to draw a side view of a horse.

Start by asking, "What shapes are there in a horse?"

The body and head are ovals.

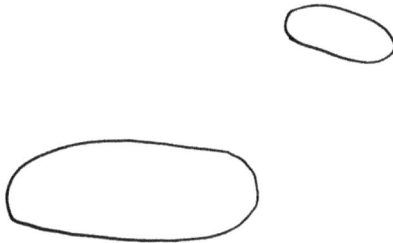

The legs and neck are triangles and rectangles.

The lower legs are triangles.

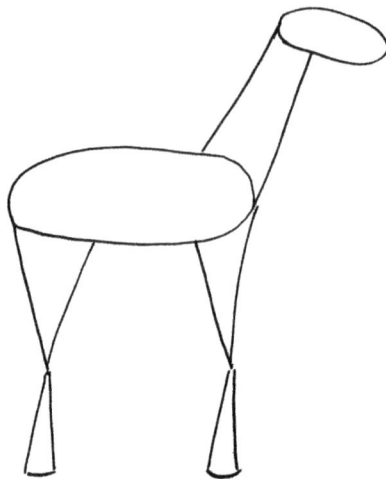

Finally, add the small circles for the body and head.

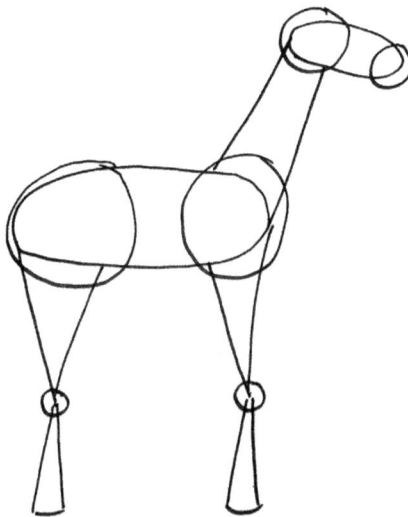

Put these together, and finish off the last shapes.

See how, using only shapes, you've created the simple framework of the horse? This allows you to see what you need to reshape or resize. If you were an artist, you'd then sketch in the rest of the body, rubbing out what you didn't need.

It's pretty simple. But imagine what your horse would have looked like if you hadn't use the shapes method.

Some other shapes that are great to use when you're drawing include:

~ Speech bubbles

~ Arrows

~ Hearts

These simple icons can add wonderful context to words. Combining shapes and words together is a great way to declutter information, make powerful points, and – importantly – save a whole bunch of time.

The Ogre's last stand: drawing people

Lastly, I want to take you to the Wild, Wild West of drawing. It's the place my clients are always most scared of going. It's dusty, the wind blows strong, the cacti are sharp, and it's where the Ogres run wild.

Let me introduce you to the art of drawing people, which is almost everyone's pain point. It's also the Ogre's chief weapon in proving how uncreative you are. "You're not creative," it sniggers. "You can only draw stick figures."

But just like drawing a horse, drawing people is about drawing what you see, instead of what you think you see. And when you think about what you actually see, no one really looks like this.

Think about it: Mr Stick Figure above has a head like a bowling ball, a neck like a giraffe, no shoulders, and no hips. His legs come out at 45 degree angles from the bottom of his spine, and his arms are at right angles to his chest. If he needs to pick something up, he'll have issues.

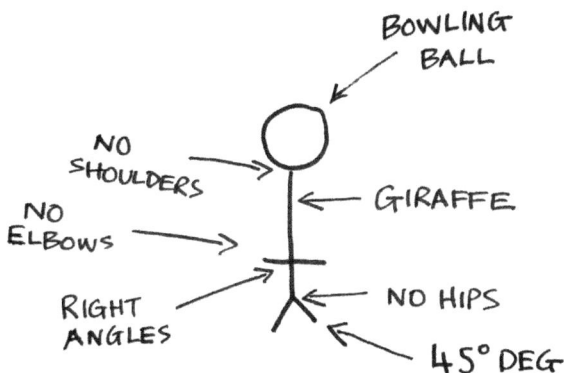

In other words: Mr Stick Figure is a bit of a weirdo.

And because he looks so weird, you don't feel much of a connection with him. So your Ogre then sends you a little message about how crap your drawing is.

With just a few small shifts, though, you can make Mr Stick Figure look a whole lot more like someone you and the people you're communicating with can understand. The great news is that you only need 10% realism for your brain to recognise what you are drawing. And 10% realism is easy when you use the right structure.

Stick with the bowling ball for a head, sure. But then actually give the figure a body. Start with the shoulders and hips and then join them to create a torso. Hurrah, this person is starting to look real.

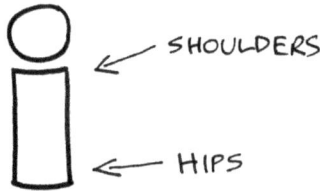

And they always need long limbs. Always. And make the limbs come from the corners of the torso, not halfway across or down.

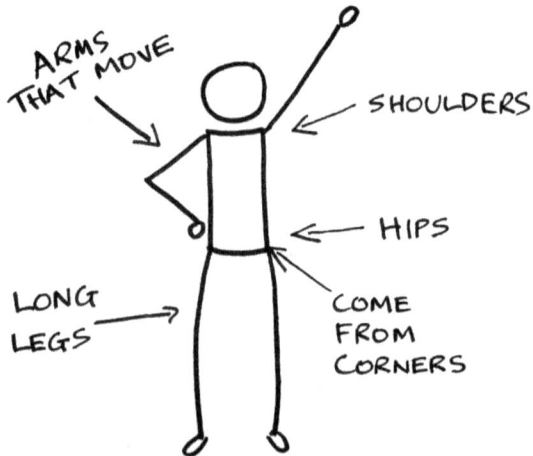

If you're drawing a woman, add a ponytail or long hair. I appreciate that this may be a stereotype, but I've tested the effect with audiences, and it works well for easy recognition and simplicity.

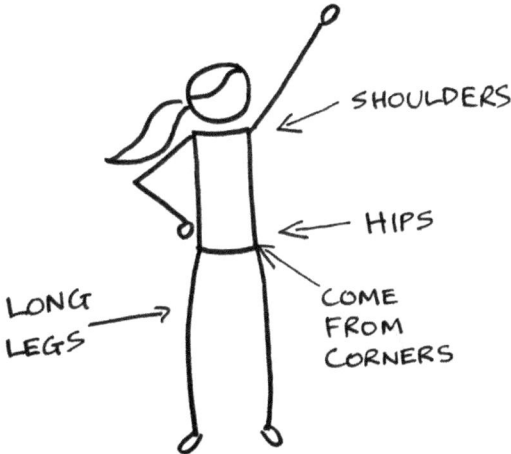

If you want to draw a group of people, start with the heads, then add some bodies underneath.

Now, ask yourself: if you were walking down the street and walked past both your original stick figure, and these slightly more detailed figures, who would you be most likely to hang out with?

Remember these things about drawing anything:

~ Practice makes perfect. So practise.

~ You'll make loads of mistakes, and that's OK.

~ Use the KISS theory: Keep It Simple Stupid. Always ask, "What's the simplest way that I can visualise this?"

~ Henri Matisse said, "Creativity takes courage." Drawing takes a little courage as well; but the more you do it, the less courage it takes.

Now you have the basic skills to start visualising and shifting your thinking (and your team's), and a wonderful tool to help you easily communicate with a wide audience. You have a way to make complex problems simple; and importantly, a way to get to where you need to at speed.

Whatever you draw, make it easy for yourself and your audience by **labelling everything**. What looks like an orange to one person may be a gold coin to someone else – and those different interpretations can completely change the context of your drawing.

Finally, don't be shy of colour. As a minimum, when you create a flowchart, use at least three colours:

~   One colour for the drawings

~   Another for the labels you give your drawings

~   A third for the arrows that connect everything

This will make it easy for your audience to navigate the drawing, and get your point across more easily.

So next time you're stuck, or want to shift your thinking, reach for your pen and say, "Let's draw this out to get a different view".

Keep your baby warm

Once you're producing mock-ups or prototypes, it's time to think about an incubator.

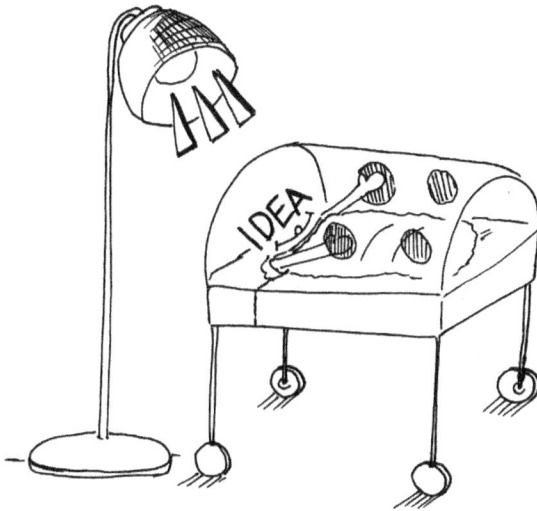

When you prototype, you bring an idea to life. New ideas are precious little things. When they're young and just starting to form, they're like infants. And just like with infants, you need to consider certain things to help them survive.

WHEN
you prototype,
you bring an idea
to life.

For example:

~ They need to be kept warm.

~ They need to be looked after.

~ They need to be checked on regularly.

~ They need to have their vital stats checked: How is the idea looking? How is it forming? Based on what you know, is there anything else you can do to make this idea healthy and help it to grow?

~ They need to be kept safe from marauding hallway vultures of negativity and escaped Ogres until they're big enough to stand on their own two feet and look after themselves.

Just like you'd treat an infant differently to the way you'd treat a teenager, you need to treat your ideas differently in their infant stage.

So why use an "incubator" for ideas?

~ It tells the Ogre to stay where it is.

~ It sends a message that things need to be a little different.

~ It's a time for constant iteration.

~ It sends a signal that you're still in a building, exploring, and feedback stage.

The way you think in this incubation phase needs to be different. The language that you use here is different. The lights are a little softer. It has a special set of rules just like nurturing an infant does. You don't send your infant to pick up milk from the shops in their first week at home from hospital. You don't scold them if they're back late and then follow that with a hundred push ups, just to toughen them up. Like with an infant, you don't want to be too hard on your idea yet.

This is the stage in the innovation process before you pitch the idea. It's a time for further exploration, more feedback, and some great thinking. It's a time for play, and a time for tinkering.

Note: this "incubation" phase isn't about putting your head in the sand and ignoring the world around you. Yes, when you initially explore a problem, an "all ideas are good ideas" approach is fine. By the time you get to this stage, however, your ideas need to be facing commercial reality. A car made of pumpkins sounds awesome to a farmer who has loads of pumpkins and spare tyres. But the commercial reality is that a pumpkin car is probably not what the market needs. A culture of innovation doesn't ignore that you need to provide real-world solutions to real-world problems.

So what are the 'do's and 'don't's of incubating your idea?

Things that will push your idea out into the cold:

~ **Ripping your idea to shreds.** Absolutely, be prepared to get and give honest feedback. Just don't be like a crowd of seven-year-old kids at a birthday party, jumping on a dropped lolly bag and pulling it to shreds.

~ **Bringing in a group of 50 people to review your idea.** There are plenty of Ogres out there, and they'll all love to tell you how shitty your idea is. Ogres love company, so keep the groups small and diverse to drive a richer feedback conversation.

~ **Taking the piss out of your idea (or anyone else's).** It's easy to revert to saying, "Oh, it was just a stupid idea anyway. What do I know?" the moment something doesn't work out as you'd intended. Once you let the Ogre back in by mocking what you've done, though, your culture of innovation starts to die.

~ **Only looking at the failures.** I'm not saying you should wear blinkers and pretend that everything is awesome. But don't lock yourself into only seeing what's wrong either. Keep your eyes wide open, and keep looking for what's great and what else you need to do or add to your idea.

~ **Forgetting about your idea.** Most of us have heard a story about someone who had an idea for 'X', but never did anything about it. Before they knew it, someone else was doing something with that exact same idea.

I was talking about the HBO TV comedy "The Flight of the Concords" one day in a workshop. It's a very funny show about two young New Zealanders trying to make it big in New York with their folk band. Then I had a long conversation during a lunch break with someone who said he'd thought up the same idea as the show.

It was the weirdest conversation: he felt really aggrieved that someone else had used his idea. I wasn't sure what to say. Bad luck? Commiserations? He just kept saying, "I had that idea!"

I felt like I was an inadvertent counsellor with no real experience in this role. I ended up saying, "I guess you'll just have to be cool with the fact that you didn't make a TV show, so you can't be too upset about their success," with a wincing smile.

Remember: an idea is nothing unless it moves forward. Innovation is *not* just a bunch of ideas sitting around somewhere gathering dust.

Things that will keep your idea cosy and warm while it grows:

~ **Starting to test your idea.** Ask yourself and your team:

  - What are our users saying?

  - Is this solving the problem that we thought it would?

  - What's great about this idea?

  - What else does this idea need?

  - Are there any other indicators from the market?

~ **Exploring the next steps.** Ask:

  - How do we take this idea further?

  - What other features should we add?

  - What priorities we should set?

  - What are the simplest, cheapest steps to make this a minimum viable product to test further?

  - What's involved in making this happen?

  - Who's involved in this?

~ **Get feedback from those around you.** Get feedback from your market and your customers. Record that feedback, and use the data to drive your decisions. Your target market can offer the best possible feedback; and you and your team know your target market better than anyone. (Or at least you *should*. If not, get busy.)

Get different people – remember the naive experts we talked about in the last chapter – to look at your idea. Embrace the diversity that's already there in your company, remembering that feedback from people with different backgrounds and job titles is essential.

~ **Embrace Iteration.** Keep on constantly tinkering, testing, learning, and improving. At every turn, there will be learning and knowledge. Use this new knowledge as a spark to do more and make your idea even better. If the first version isn't right, keep at it.

Whilst iterating an innovative product should be ongoing, the prototyping and incubation phases are the right time to start it.

One of the great learnings I had with writing this book is that my market is alive with insight and feedback – and is more than happy to provide it. Your idea and your market's insight is a winning mix that sits in that Innovation Sweet Spot.

So treat your idea well. Put it in the incubator; and don't stop testing it, getting feedback on it, and creating new iterations until it's just right.

Framework #6:
Pitch it

When you pitch an idea, it gets even more real. This is the point when you *must* put some skin in the game. You have to give your idea a name.

This is when you need a big dose of bravery – after all, you're putting some of your heart and soul on the line. You'll bring up the nasty concept of change; and despite every indication from your market that change is needed, there'll be plenty of dinosaurs within your organisation who don't like it.

"We're cold-blooded," those dinosaurs insist. "We don't like change in our dinosaur world. Have you seen what those warm-blooded mammals are doing on the next floor? Those upstarts. It's ridiculous!" No, these dinosaurs don't like new concepts, new products or new ideas.

Remember: there's a reason that dinosaurs don't roam the hills any more. A new idea represents a change in the status quo; and that can be a little uncomfortable for the "We like it just the way it is" creatures. (Let's be honest: at least initially, it can be a little uncomfortable for the rest of us too.)

Why is pitching so important?

Pitching an idea is the perfect way to bring the world and that idea together. Pitching is when all your actions towards innovation suddenly become real. It's the first step in the process of testing your idea commercially. Remember the pumpkin car I talked about in the last chapter?

In a culture of innovation – one with a constant stream of market-leading thinking, great ideas and those thousand little lightbulb moments happening all the time – there *has* to be a constant stream of great pitches. Those pitches can happen anywhere – they don't have to take place in front of a formal panel. You can pitch peer-to-peer, to your team, your partners, or fellow leaders. Regardless, as a leader, you need to create an environment where pitching is normal, and people don't just let their ideas sit idly and gather dust.

TV programs like *Shark Tank* or *Dragon's Den* have made the idea of pitching a whole lot more familiar (and popular) – and they've done so for a good reason. All ideas need that dose of commercial reality, and pitching an idea is its first introduction to reality. Pitching provides the diverse feedback and fresh perspective that your team needs. When you pitch, that real-world feedback lights up your senses.

In my Innovation Workshops or Hackathaons, pitching is the acid test for everyone's ideas. It makes everyone sit right up and smell the coffee. (Although… don't worry if *Shark Tank* sounds too scary. We go with more of a *Dolphin Pool* scenario: similar, but friendlier.)

Pitching also provides some pressure to ensure your best self turns up. You know that if you turn up and do a shitty job, it can send a message to others that you don't believe in the ideas that you or your team are pitching.

This stage is when the pieces of the puzzle start to come together. The great news is that much of the hard work is already done:

~   You're already got really clear on the problem you're trying to solve.

~   You've finished exploring different ways to fix this problem.

~   You've got plenty of feedback, and done plenty of research. Your idea has already been explored by a hugely diverse audience.

~   You've also prototyped it and gathered further feedback and insight. So you're already convinced that the idea is workable.

Next, you have to get real, back yourself, and just pitch. How, you ask? You can do it in all kinds of different ways. The key is to just do it. For example, you could try to:

~   Pitch it to yourself in the mirror.

~   Pitch it to your cat.

~   Pitch it to a few teammates.

~   Pitch it at the pub.

~   Pitch it to your Nan.

~   Pitch it for real.

~   Just pitch.

Get real and pitch it

What are the elements of a great pitch?

- *Use the KISS theory: Keep it Simple, Stupid. It's a great design principle, a great life principle, and a fantastic principle to use for pitching.*

- *Be really clear on the problem you're solving.*

- *Don't just hand in a written proposal: stand on your feet and deliver it.*

- *Use a human-centred approach, and put yourself in your listener's shoes. No one likes to be bored senseless. Make your pitch interesting, and tell a great story.*

- *Use multiple forms of sensory engagement. Remember, you can draw now.*

- *Get busy and – like Nike says – just DO it.*

How to deal with feedback

What if you get feedback that isn't 100% encouraging? If so, embrace it: there's gold in them there feedback hills!

A life lesson from pitching

When I was a young artist, fresh out of university, I showed my artwork to countless commercial galleries. I was relatively bolshy about it: I'd just wander in with my portfolio and try to grab a chat. (This was back in the old-school days when you still used a physical portfolio, not just a hard drive with your images on it).

I remember the owner of the gallery that eventually represented me saying that I was ahead of most of my peers. Why? Simply because I was there in the gallery, pitching my work.

I received loads of feedback on that portfolio. A lot of it was negative, which could be really deflating. I worked on developing the mindset that all feedback was useful. Even the galleries that weren't interested in my work gave me great information that I could use. They made points about:

- *My presentation*
- *What didn't work for them*
- *The timing for shows*
- *The colours they hated (and why)*
- *What their clients wanted*
- *Who else I could go and see*

There was value everywhere if I chose to take it. Every pitch, every subsequent rejection, and every learning I chose to take from it made me smarter for the next one. It was real-world feedback from my market, and all those different perspectives were invaluable.

At last, I connected with a commercial gallery where the director said, "I haven't been as impressed with a painting like this for a long, long time. Bring in some more work and let's talk." And finally I was away. All of the feedback I'd received before that point put me in the best space to deliver for this new gallery.

What about great feedback?

Of course, you need to be OK with negative feedback, but what about if you get the opposite? What if your idea gets people out of their chairs? Author Scott Berkun says that you must always be ready for a positive response too. Be prepared to take your idea to the next level, and don't look shocked if you hear someone say, "I like it!"

As I did when I got my eventual "yes" at the art gallery, you need to have a plan to move forward. Understand what your next step will be. Make sure you know who you'll involve to get things happening.

PITCHING
is when all your actions towards innovation suddenly become real.

You also need to encourage and reward your team for pitching their ideas (more on this in the next section). Team meetings should always include a pitch element. It could be an elevator pitch (10 seconds), an elevator pitch for a much taller building (30–60 seconds) or a five-minute elevator pitch for a skyscraper in Dubai.

Regardless of the length, make sure pitching just feels normal.

As the leader of a truly innovative team, you need to encourage your team to pitch all the time. There are brilliant perspectives waiting to be heard. There are divergent views ready to combine to create something greater, and these need to be shared.

"I like" and "I wish"

To ensure that you incorporate the divergent views that will help to build on pitched ideas (rather than killing them), it's important to adopt a different feedback language. Remember that people immediately notice whatever's crap about something a long time before they notice what they like about it. This is when the Ogre (remember this loser?) rubs its hands together and smiles content-edly, knowing it's managed to kill someone's creativity yet again.

Tom and David Kelley, authors of *Creative Confidence* recommend using two types of language when hearing a pitch and giving feedback:

~ Here's what I LIKE about your idea…

~ Here's what I WISH your idea had…

Using this kind of language doesn't mean you're being soft and cuddly about everything. It's just a choice of words that will take ideas forward instead of blocking them.

As we spoke about in Chapter 8, language is a huge part of a successful innovation model. That's why you start with, "Here's what I LIKE about your idea," first; and only then follow up with "Here's what I WISH it had…" That way, you encourage the idea to continue to develop, rather than stopping it in its tracks. This creates confidence in the person pitching; and as a bonus, confuses the hell out of the Ogre to ensure it stays quiet.

Here's how to get people pitching as if they were born to do it:

~ Make the pitching process an enjoyable, everyday part of your culture.

~ Pitch as many ideas as possible.

~ Hear as many ideas as possible.

~ Use the feedback to improve and modify ideas.

~ If you encounter a roadblock, use any feedback you get to course correct.

~ Pitch for feedback to each other and to your customers.

~ Pitch to keep focused and excited.

Be brave, keep it real, and keep pitching. A culture of innovation awaits – one that produces market-leading thinking, ideas, products and results.

Recognition and rewards in the new world

The term "New World" conjures up images of explorers sailing away from Europe 300 years ago. Families all wave good bye at the port as they watch barrel after barrel of rum being loaded onto the ship, wondering if they'll ever see those sailors again. Meanwhile, the sailors, who are mostly delighted with the amount of rum, also wonder what treasures they might bring back from other lands. They're feeling excited, nervous, and full of possibilities.

Sound familiar?

You might not be sailing off overseas, but as a leader driving a culture of innovation, you're probably heading into new territory. That requires new thinking and new behaviours, which involves risk and bravery – both of which will drive a culture of innovation, and need to be recognised and rewarded.

In my research for this book, I had many conversations with senior leaders that started with me asking, "What's stopping your company from innovating?"

Time and time again, the response was, "Our KPIs just don't reward this type of behaviour. Yes, we say we value innovation, but there's no incentive for anyone to be involved."

Recognise that you may *literally* be the first team to truly embrace an innovation mindset in your company. And you know that there will be at lest some unknowns, since innovation is never linear. So ask yourself:

~   How will you recognise and reward the great behaviours that develop a culture of innovation?

~   How will you recognise the "getting-off-your-arse" behaviour that develops market-leading thinking?

~   How will you reward the rapid experiments that lead to great ideas?

~   How will you recognise the team members who are always pitching new insights and ideas?

~   How will you reward the learnings from, dare I say it, *failure?*

Daniel Pink gives a great TED Talk on the power of motivation, and how this has changed over the last 40-50 years as the role of work has shifted. As we've moved from the industrialised age, our work no longer involves repeating the same task over and over. The carrot-and-stick type reward might work OK in linear "if you do x then y will happen" work. But it simply isn't suited to a culture of innovation.

In a podcast interview with the *Harvard Business Review*'s Katherine Bell, Pink says,

> *"[In] work that is more conceptual, that requires big picture thinking, that requires a greater degree of creativity, that requires solving more complicated, complex challenges, the if-then motivators don't work very well at all. And that's not even a close call on the science. The behavioural science is very, very clear that – give people those kinds of motivators for creative, conceptual, complex tasks, and they will often underperform."*

The rewards and recognition for a culture of innovation need to be a little different from the standard "hit target/get reward" or "make a thousand widgets/get a bigger Christmas party" type incentives.

You know from experience that developing a new culture is *not* an overnight thing. It takes time. All large companies have values or behaviours that they want their staff to model as part of their culture. Creativity and innovation need to become part of those values.

If you recognise and reward the great people in your team for innovative behaviour, you'll build a culture of innovation. And *then* you'll start to turbocharge everything.

As your starting point, recognise and reward:

- *Team members who constantly pitch ideas.*
- *Networking and collaboration between diverse teams and employees to take an idea further.*
- *Fresh insight and research into customers' problems (remember that innovation starts with problems, not ideas).*
- *Teams that take a different path in trying to solve those problems.*
- *Ideas that didn't work but produced learning to be used elsewhere (yes, a little fail!)*
- *People who've taken on an interesting hobby or something outside of work.*
- *A team member who does something new to bring freshness and new thinking into your company.*
- *Transparency and people being prepared to openly and honestly say that something isn't working. Great ideas happen when opposing opinions bump heads.*

McKinsey & Company say that leaders should think about two types of metrics around innovation: financial (such as the percentage of total revenue from new products), and behavioural[1].

How are other companies doing this differently?

~ Christa Carone, former Xerox CMO, said that in her time at Xerox, they held Beaker Awards[2]. (Remember Dr Bunsen Honeydew's crazy lab assistant from the Muppets who kept experimenting and blowing himself up?) These were awarded to marketing team members in honour of small wins that they hoped would be game-changers down the road. Carone said that the awards were, "… given to marketing teams who stepped out of the box, and created compelling campaigns or activities that are bold and believable, unexpected and relevant."

~ 3M has established that at least 30% of its revenues should be generated from products launched within the last four years[3]. They also allow scientists/inventors to have a dual career ladder that enables them to keep moving up without becoming managers.

~ At Google X, failure is rewarded[4] (yes, I know that's a hard one).

~ Google actually replaced its compensation-based Founder Awards with experience-based rewards[5].

~ The Tata Group has innovation awards that include recognition for[6]:

  - Innovative business ideas that have not yet been tried.

  - Sincere, audacious attempts to create a major innovation that failed to get the desired results.

Recognise and reward often, and make it fun! Because every company has their own individual culture (and innovation is divergent anyway), the reward and recognition system you implement will be unique to *your* organisation. Even within your company, different things will motivate different people. So seek feedback from your teams on what works, test it often, learn from any failures, and continue onwards and upwards.

The future looks very bright – so what happens now?

Framework #7: Repeat

The process of innovation is never-ending; and it requires a never-ending curiosity and energy to make great stuff happen. That's why "Repeat" is the new mantra for a culture of innovation. When you keep repeating the things that have brought you this far, even greater things are possible.

Once you start to repeat, things also start to look different. They start to transform.

But this only happens with *deliberate* repetition. You can't just innovate once, try a few things from this book, and then call it done. Innovation is a process that takes time, commitment, and sometimes a willingness to move way out of your comfort zone and stay there.

It takes guts.

If you thought a culture of innovation could happen while you stayed part of the status quo, this is your worst nightmare. (Also, you haven't been paying attention to the previous twelve chapters.)

But if you're willing to do what it takes to create and grow an organisational culture of innovation, you'll have to embrace the word "repeat".

What does repetition do for you?

It literally transforms your people

Think of a "before and after" experience you've had. It might have been heading off on a two-week trek in the Andes mountains. You knew you'd need to massively improve your fitness level, so you enrolled in a high-intensity fitness boot camp that ran for three months before you left.

Before the boot camp began, your fitness instructor took a photo of you. Then, over the next few months, you got up early four times a week, and gave each workout your everything. By the end of it, you were feeling good, and your energy was popping all over the place.

Before you finished up, your instructor took another photo. And when you compared your before and after photos, you couldn't believe it. There'd been a major transformation. Not only did you feel great, but you looked great too. You knew you'd smash that trek.

That's the level of transformation that repetition can create in your team (although possibly with fewer muscles).

So ask yourself what the "before and after" shot for your team and organisation could be once you embrace your curiosity and develop a culture of innovation.

~ What will be different with your people?

~ What will the change look and feel like for them?

~ What will it look and feel like for you?

Great, great things are possible with a more creative and open mindset. Possibilities are everywhere when you get past whatever your Ogre is telling you.

This isn't a book on breaking through limiting beliefs per se, but I truly believe that you can't have both a culture of innovation AND limiting beliefs about your (and your team's) creative potential. People's belief in their lack of creative ability is a heavy burden to bear.

As Gandhi said:

> *"Your beliefs become your thoughts,*
> *your thoughts become your words,*
> *your words become your actions,*
> *your actions become your habits,*
> *your habits become your values,*
> *your values become your destiny."*

A culture of innovation is not about making everyone in your organisation into the next Andy Warhol or Thomas Edison. Instead, it's about enabling them to tap into the innovative potential they already have to make new connections. It's about helping them tap into their existing power to make better choices. Their ability to say, "Hell yeah, let's give this a go!" with gusto. Their ability to say, "I'm confident that I have the creative power to kick some arse with this problem," and mean it.

And then, it's about helping them to do it over and over again, as you continue to create a legacy and solve great challenges.

When people get rid of their Ogres and reconnect with their creative potential, they immediately start out on the path to greater possibilities. It's as though you gain a whole new team. Combining this rediscovered innovative spirit with confidence in their creative abilities and their existing fantastic analytical and logical skills is a potent recipe for success. Great people exist already, right in front of you. There's no such thing as "uncreative people". There are only people who haven't fulfilled their creative potential.

Imagine a team that can:

~ Be more productive

~ Have better ideas

~ Easily tap into fresh thinking

~ Be more accepting of each others' thinking

~ Act more collaboratively

~ Collectively build on ideas, rather than shutting them down

~ Come to work with a fresh smile

~ Feel inspired about what can happen that day

~ Bring ten amazing perspectives on a problem together as one, rather than bringing one or two perspectives with eight passengers

This isn't a recipe for making everything perfect, of course. Despite your best efforts, difficult people will still be difficult, and some people will always have to be dragged, kicking and screaming. I can't claim that a team's new-found creative spirit will change those people, or that everyone will suddenly become wildly enthused about the new way of doing things.

With luck, sooner rather than later, those people will come on board – that or they'll decide they don't want to be somewhere that fresh thinking is the norm. (Perhaps they'd rather be onscreen in David Attenborough's *Walking with Dinosaurs*). What I *do* know is that a company with a culture of innovation will attract great people. Those people will want to be somewhere that innovation is the norm, not just an afterthought.

Keep in mind that intentional, repeated innovation is not about creativity or experimenting for the sake of it. It's not about riding around the office on a unicycle (or wearing your cap backwards) because you're just so damn crazy. Neither is it about spending every lunchtime playing air hockey from a repossessed, crocheted bean bag. And it's certainly not about only eating organic kale and Mayan quinoa salads.

Instead, it's about that constant supply of fresh thinking and the thousand little lightbulb moments that can drive your business forward. It's also about being proud and brave enough to share that thinking – and doing all this repeatedly. And that's exactly what attracts the great people who'll complement the awesome team you already have.

As a leader, you're in your role because you do a fantastic job. The piece you can add to your existing success is an innovation mindset. Just imagine what could happen if you tapped into that. It's already there, and it's free.

Imagine the potential in reigniting whole-brain thinking in both yourself AND your team. Seriously, the possibilities are just outrageous. You'd end up leading a team of superhumans. Can you feel yourself jumping out of your chair with excitement at that thought? Climb a little higher, stand on your chair, and scream aloud. (Actually, no, sit down. Health and Safety regulations probably forbid it.)

Remember that no one has a monopoly on ideas.

The key to making that superhuman team work is to remember that fresh thinking is *not* just the domain of the few. You need to encourage absolutely everyone to use their creative potential.

To open their eyes and trust in their own talent. To contribute ideas, and to be bold in their thinking when it's required.

You already know that your people are your greatest asset. Their knowledge, skill and drive will take your company forward. They'll drive your organisation's ability to delight your customers. Any success you have comes down to them. Their (currently unused) innovation potential will only complement this. With great people and a culture that embraces innovation, you can tackle whatever the market throws at you.

Keep repeating the process, and the problem of disruption becomes *totally* last year.

Transform your business

Any company can achieve a culture of innovation, because the principles to build it are universal. Everyone is capable of learning this type of attitude, outlook, and behaviour – and when they do, it will transform your business.

A new response to problems

Imagine that there's a very important team meeting coming up about a major piece of work that you're tendering for. This work could solve significant problems, and take your organisation into a new market with plenty of scope for years of ongoing work. This market has been on your radar for a few years now, so it's a sector you'd really like to crack.

There'll also be major competition on the tender, and the client's looking for something transformative and fresh. There's plenty of pressure, which is nothing new. However, there is something new in your approach.

Your team comes into the room ready to go – not just present physically, but really, truly ready to go. Things are a little different from the way they used to be. Everyone now walks around with their eyes wide open, seeing things that they used to walk past, and actively seeking stimulation to keep their thinking fresh.

Ideas flow thick and fast. Many of them seem "out there," but instead of immediately discarding them, your team quickly builds on them. They display and record their ideas on the wall in various formats. You watch as each team member contributes:

- *Moonchild February Jones, your youngest team member and funky millennial, takes everyone though an app on her phone that's immediately relevant. She's at the heart of the conversation because she brings a completely different perspective from everyone else.*

- *Sally dashes out of the room and returns again with a magazine that's relevant too.*

- *Rio highlights a company doing some great work that mirrors the challenges your client is facing.*

- *Bruce shows a few YouTube clips that caught his eye, and offers insight.*

- *Levi's drawing and then collating visual ideas on the wall to map out your client's current journey, and identify where they're getting stuck.*

- *Eden describes her time in Japan last year, where she saw some awesome branding around a similar theme. She finds a picture on her phone (saved in her "Awesome ideas – Japan" folder) and projects it onto the wall screen.*

- *Ryan – the team's resident introvert – has spent most of the time outside of the room in silence, because everyone understands that that's where his best thinking happens. He comes back in with some great information, and creates a flow diagram of what he's put together.*

Everyone puts their ideas forward quickly. You can feel the buzz in the room, and the creativity and conversation both flow freely.

After 90 minutes, this room is a different place. People pop their heads in the door to get a sense of what's going on, and to be part of the conversation. Word has spread that your team is a little different, with a very different energy. Your results are better, so you're seen as the go-to group. People seek you out for your fresh insight, and your unique outlook is contagious.

The creative energy on the tender project ensures that it moves fast, especially compared to eighteen months ago. Meetings back then were productive, but they were nothing like this. Everyone now contributes, and the business results of tapping into fresh thinking have been unbelievable. Everyone has amazing insights and perspectives that are unique to them, and they share it all freely. It's like someone turned on the ideas tap, and the fresh thinking is flowing out in torrents.

Open-minded, adventurous people are now working hand-in-hand with logical, analytical, and reliable ones. People with these different thinking and behaviour styles are working with *each other, rather than trying to dominate each other.*

You've found the Innovation Sweet Spot.

I do a lot of work in the mining and resources sector, which provides a great example of how behaviour and attitude can become embedded in a culture. This sector has a particularly strong culture around safety, because if they get something wrong, someone ends up dead. Lives get ruined and families are torn apart without a culture of safety.

So if someone sees something that doesn't look right on a work site, they don't just rush in to fix it without thinking. Instead, they first consider the safety implications. If something must be moved, they think it through. Before anyone starts a task, they do a full safety brief, even for something an outsider would consider relatively benign. Whilst this feels strange for anyone outside the mining and resources sector, within the industry, it's just standard.

The thought of *not* doing a safety assessment simply doesn't exist. Everyone wants to go home alive, to be a great parent to their kids and live a long life. This behaviour and mindset is practiced so often, it's normal. It's not just part of the culture, it *is* the culture. It's like the Bruce Lee quote, "Knowing is not enough, we must apply. Willing is not enough, we must do."

Everyone who comes into a mining and resources organisation understands that safety is non-negotiable. They also understand the minimum standard for success, and they *practise* that behaviour. The same thing can happen in your organisation too, if you keep bringing creativity and innovation behaviours into play and normalising them.

> *"What we've done to encourage innovation is make it ordinary."* – Craig Wynett, Chief Creative Officer, Procter and Gamble

Don't think for a minute that innovation can't become part of your company's culture, or that it can't become your new normal. You know that innovation is important: you just need to move from knowing to doing. Of course, it will require a shift; but repeating even the smallest steps and actions can make a huge difference.

Remember that once you repeat steps and actions regularly, you normalise them. What becomes normal becomes your culture. It becomes what people participate in when they join. It becomes why people *want* to join.

A lack of fresh ideas and a culture of staleness don't stop people from going home alive. However, those things *do* create a mindset of surviving instead of thriving. They mean that your organisation doesn't head in the right direction. They also mean your organisation can't make the impact that it should.

So make a culture of fresh thinking your new normal. Make a culture of building on ideas instead of killing them your new standard. Create a default mindset of "yes" rather than "no;" and make that something that everyone is part of throughout the company.

Innovation isn't just a value on a poster. It's something that everyone can't wait to be a part of. Keep repeating it.

Transform your life

Let's be clear. An innovation mindset isn't just about your people or your business. It's about you as well. You're important. Your life is important. The quality of your life, and the quality of your interactions with the world are important too. The quality of the legacy that you leave behind you is *vitally* important. So finding

IMAGINE
the potential in reigniting whole-brain thinking in both yourself AND your team.

your creative heartbeat and your innovation mindset is at the centre of any impact that you make.

Your creative potential shouldn't be something you *used* to have. Think back to when you were younger. Don't stop at eighteen years old: go right back to when you were four or five – when a cardboard box wasn't a box or recycling. *It was potential.* It was a rocket ship flying to the moon. It was a castle that had to be protected, or a boat to be sailed across the lounge room full of pirates. It was part of a body to be joined up to other cardboard boxes to make the world's largest caterpillar. It was a portal to another universe.

Remember those times? The mindset that saw cardboard boxes as nothing less than possibilities is the mindset you, your team, and your organisation need to thrive in an ever-shifting market place. Rediscovering and then using those creative abilities can only mean great things. Having an active imagination gives you that

"What if?" outlook, rather than a "Let's not" one. Fresh thinking opens more possibilities across your entire life.

~ **Holidays look different.** You ask your family, "Where shall we adventure this year?'

~ **Weekends take on a different slant.** You decide you're finally going to work out how to use that gift you received five years ago.

~ **Hobbies become much more interesting.** You decide to try something new, and feel comfortable knowing you won't be good at it the first time around.

~ **Family time takes on a whole new approach.** You come up with a multitude of ideas other than staring at the TV.

At the end of the art programs I run, there are always a few people who say they're going to go home, find the canvas that's kicking around in their garage, and *paint*. And I always get excited to hear this for a couple of reasons:

~ **Firstly, I just love the idea of someone painting.** There's absolute joy to be had in creating and seeing colour come to life; and the positive impacts of happiness and joy are immense.

~ **Beyond that, though, it's not just about creating a painting.** It's the start of someone getting comfortable with using their natural creative abilities. Every stroke of the brush that that person makes is another step in silencing their Ogre.

Creating a painting is a metaphor for trying anything new, taking any risk, or venturing anywhere outside your comfort zone. It could be going somewhere new on the weekend, or doing something different with the kids. It could be reading a new book in a genre you wouldn't normally pick up. It could be learning something new at work. Or yes, it could be pitching that idea you've had in your back pocket for the last two years.

Your life until now has given you stories, experiences, and mindsets, which in turn have given you the blinkers you use to look at the world. Reigniting your creative spirit will help you to shift those blinkers and see things differently.

Think of your bucket list. Most people don't leave their jobs to tick off a bucket list that looks like this:

1.   Be as boring as possible

2.   Learn matchstick-counting

3.   Settle down

4.   Watch endless TV test patterns

5.   Memorise government legislation

Instead, their bucket list looks more like this:

1.   Travel the world

2.   Write a novel

3.   Run a winery

4.   Learn photography

5.   Jump naked out of a plane

With the *possible* exception of No #5, the items on most people's bucket lists are experiences that let them re-embrace their imagination and nurture their long-lost creative souls. Don't wait until you retire: start that process right now.

Look back, look forwards

If you've read this far, you've come a long way. You now know that creativity is natural, normal, and something you have in abundance.

So for this exercise, make a list of five things that you'll do over the next six months to embrace your creativity. Treat it like a six-month bucket list, with items that you've always wanted to do, but didn't have the creative confidence to try. Or perhaps include things you'd just never thought of because your blinkers wouldn't let you.

Aim high, and avoid the "sweep the drive" type activities. Include things that will take you into your creative stretch zone (also known as the "place where good shit happens" zone).

Put a date against each item, and get an accountability buddy to keep you on track. Once you've crossed everything off, make your next list and repeat. Don't aim for one final bucket list – have several to develop your creative spirit.

Remember that the only difference between a creative and a non-creative person is that creative people do creative things. Their creativity doesn't come from luck or pure genetics. It comes from repetition. Creative people do things that constantly fan their curiosity, stretch their imagination, and develop their creativity. The end result is that they can transfer these skills across everything that they do.

It feels good to create. Life wasn't made to be lived constantly in your comfort zone. Find your creative outlet and go for it. There's so much joy to be had from a more open mindset. An ability to look at life from all angles. An ability to bring something to life that didn't exist before.

The father of brainstorming, Alex F. Osborn, said, "Creative imagination, the lamp that lit the world, can light our lives." You haven't just lit a lamp: you've bought a set of spotlights, and placed them on the front of a jet plane. There's so much light now that you probably need expensive sunglasses. Your eyes are open to great new things. Your possibility radar has become much, much bigger.

Hit repeat, then get ready: the most interesting (and amazing) times are ahead.

Where to now?

One small step. I'm sure you've heard the quote attributed to Chinese philosopher Lao Tzu: "A journey of a thousand miles begins with a single step". Nowhere is this truer than when you're developing a culture of innovation. A culture of a thousand little lightbulb moments starts with just one spark… and then lights begin to appear everywhere.

So just get started. Take one small step. Even small actions can produce ripple effects. More and more small actions start to produce something much bigger. You move from a ripple to a splash. The splash gets a little bigger, and starts to look something like a wave. The waves get bigger… and before you know it, someone paddles in, stands up on their surfboard, and takes off. You are away.

You now have some great insights into what you need to do. You understand that there are creative rockets sitting under all your team members. You appreciate that you – and your team – have a lot of unused capacity.

You know the impact that a culture of innovation can have on your team and your organisation. You know that it will bring you:

~ Unique perspectives

~ Fresh thinking on old problems

~ Market-leading insight

~ True understanding and empathy for your customers

~ A feeling of enjoyment

~ Great new products and services

~ Flexibility in thinking and behaviour

~ Agile responsiveness to an ever-changing market

~ A spring in your team's steps… and possibly even an extra smile here and there

~ A buzz in the air when you walk into the office

Once a creative and innovative mindset become part of your culture, and you're taking small steps to build on it every day, your thinking will never be the same. The ideas will come. A thousand little lightbulbs will go off everywhere.

You now have a responsibility

You're responsible for keeping your imagination alive, and keeping your creative fire burning.

You've made a commitment to lead an innovative team, and enable everyone to use their creative potential. You've committed to kicking some arse in a disrupted future, and being market-ready, agile, and responsive.

Now you need to set an example.

Imagine you're starting off at that new fitness boot camp we talked about in the previous chapter. The boot camp instructor turns up ready to whip everyone into shape and help them to live a great life.

This time around, though, something doesn't look quite right. Your instructor gets visibly puffed, and doesn't actually look that fit. You easily pass them when everyone does a lap of the park. They stop to catch their breath a lot and ask everyone to go on ahead. They sweat more than everyone else… and is that a muffin top they have? You didn't pay to be run around by someone in this shape. What type of example are they setting?

Don't be that instructor for your team. Don't let yourself go creatively, or lose all your inspiration. Continue to take the steps that will keep watering your creative garden.

The author Jack London said, "You can't wait for inspiration. You have to go after it with a club." Keep trying different things, knowing that some will work better than others. Keep your eyes wide open and seek quality stimulation. Remember that great things in create great things out.

Keep seeking freshness and moving forward too. A trip to work can be a great time to spend with your eyes wide open. Your next trip through the airport screams with possibilities and insight if you

YOU'RE
responsible for keeping your imagination alive, and keeping your creative fire burning.

choose to see them. Keep looking for new ideas, and you'll find your creative flow.

You know the world is changing fast. There are new rules, new problems that need solving, new markets, and new customers. You wouldn't be reading this book if you weren't excited about what a culture of innovation could bring to your organisation.

Elon Musk said, "If you get up in the morning and think the future is going to be better, it is a bright day. Otherwise, it's not." Your organisation's future is brighter when your blinkers are off. Your future is better when your creative spirit and insight are constantly connecting with your pragmatism, logic, and experience.

I know that you're extremely time-poor. You're already busy doing a bunch of stuff. That won't change: you'll *always* be super-busy. The good news is that an innovation mindset doesn't require extra hours each week. It just requires a shift in the way you're already thinking and doing things.

~ **You already think a lot, and make tough decisions.** Now the way you think will be more expansive; and you'll keep writing down all your thoughts, sharing them, and encouraging others to build on them. Then, when it comes to making those tough decisions, you'll have a few more options to decide between.

~ **You already travel and go to a bunch of meetings.** Your eyes will now be more open to all the great ideas that exist when you travel. And the meetings you go to will be different, with a different energy, approach and outcomes. You'll end up with far less paralysis by analysis too.

~ **You've always had fantastic analytical, linear, logical and strategic skills.** Now you can use a more lateral thinking style as well when you need to; and you can frame your strategies in more visual ways that everyone can connect with.

~ **You've always connected with, and rewarded, your team.** Now you've discovered more ways to connect, and to acknowledge contribution. Plus, now that you understand that everyone in your team is sitting on a goldmine of ideas, you can acknowledge your innovators and risk-takers.

~ **You've always been super smart, talented, and results-focussed.** Now you've added another string to your bow and liberated your creativity to become ever smarter… and generate even better results.

~ **Your organisation has always said they value diversity.** You now truly understand why diversity is the greatest asset your team has. The quirkiness and uniqueness of each team member is one of the keys to their awesome thinking.

~ **There's always been an Ogre hanging about.** But now, that Ogre is fatally wounded – maybe even gone completely. It will never again wreak the damage it's been able to in the past.

~ **Things are no longer just black and white.** Black and white still exist, of course, but you also understand that you can have lime green, orange and hot pink on occasions.

Now you need to take the first step

It's just as if you wanted to go on that walk we talked about in Chapter 7…

~ You can write about the first step.

~ You can visualise the journey, and have numerous meetings about it.

~ You can have a visiting speaker talk about walking, and you can read articles on the topic.

~ You can do a presentation to your company about walking.

But none of that will *get* you anywhere. You need to actually take a step. Once you're walking, things start happening. Then, after a few more steps, it all seems a little more natural. Momentum kicks in, and you're away. Walking starts to feel normal.

So just get moving. Of course there will be stumbles and obstacles, but if you keep moving, great things are ahead. It's better to be in an expanding market and constantly evolving as you get it right, rather than staying in a contracting market with outdated thinking and behaviours.

You've chosen to be someone who isn't happy with the status quo. Someone who wants to lead an interesting life, and who aspires to lead an innovative team. You know that innovation is a *people* thing, so you want to help your team members liberate their creativity and discover their full potential. You've chosen to develop a culture that produces market-leading thinking, ideas, products, and results.

It's the start of an exciting journey. I truly wish you success, and I can't wait to read about the great things that you and your team make happen on your journey.

If you want help kickstarting your culture of innovation, please get in touch. I'd be delighted to connect and spark a multitude of little lightbulb moments with you. You can find all my contact details on the next page.

A culture of innovation is a springboard to great things for you, your team, and your organisation.

Enjoy the ride.

About Simon

Simon Banks is an author, podcaster and international speaker on creativity, innovation and design, and a happily recovering artist. He describes his geek-out spot as the intersection of creativity and design, learning, people and passion, which he sees as essential building blocks for future leaders and developing an innovative culture. His Big Why? To use his artist's curiosity combined with his 20-year corporate career to build a more creative world to enable people and business to thrive in the modern age.

Simon has substantial experience, with over 1300 events facilitated across Europe, Asia, America and Australia across a diverse array of sectors and organisations. He's worked to bring fresh thinking and innovation out of teams in companies that include: EY, Australian Ethical, Laing O'Rourke, Geoscience Australia, NAB, Economic Development Australia, Newcastle University, Google, The Australian Department of Industry, Innovation and Science, and Volkswagen.

Simon lives and breathes creativity. He has exhibited his art across the globe, has lectured at the National Gallery of England and developed programs for institutions such as The Museum of Contemporary Art in Sydney and continues to have a foot firmly planted in both the creative and corporate worlds. (It's his secret special sauce for empowering people to think differently.)

Web: www.simonbanks.com.au

Podcast: www.occupationalphilosophers.com

YouTube: www.youtube.com › simonbankstv

Contact: letschat@simonbanks.com.au

References

Chapter 2

(1.) World Economic Forum (2015). *Future of Jobs* report. p. 20.

(2.) Gray, A. (2016). *The 10 Skills You Need to Thrive in the Fourth Industrial Revolution.* Retrieved June 2017 from https://www.weforum.org/agenda/2016/01/ the-10-skills-you-need-to-thrive-in-the-fourth-industrial- revolution/

(3.) PwC (2017). *20th CEO survey.* Retrieved February 2017 from http://www.pwc.com/gx/en/ceo-agenda/ceosurvey/2017/in

(4.) Forbes (2016). *The World's Most Innovative Companies.* Retrieved May 2017 from https://www.forbes.com/ innovative-companies/#7818f8361d65

(5.) Jamrisko, M. and Lu, W. (2017). *These are the World's Most Innovative Economies.* Retrieved June 2017 from https:// www.bloomberg.com/news/articles/2017-01-17/ sweden-gains-south-korea-reigns-as-world-s-most- innovative-economies

(6.) Cornell INSEAD WIPO (2017). *The Global Innovation Index 2017: Innovation Feeding the World.* Tenth ED. Retrieved June 2017 from https://www.globalinnovationindex.org/ gii-2017-report#

(7.) Office of the Chief Economist (2016). *Australian Innovation System Report (AISR),* p. 46. Retrieved February 24, 2017 from https://industry.gov.au/Office-of-the-Chief-Economist/ Publications/Documents/Australian-Innovation- System/2016-AIS-Report.pdf

(8.) *Australian Innovation System Report* (2016). p. 40.

(9.) *Australian Innovation System Report* (2016). p. 40.

(10.) *Australian Innovation System Report* (2016). p. 48.

(11.) *Australian Innovation System Report* (2016). p. 49.

(12.) *Australian Innovation System Report* (2016). p. 42.

(13.) *Australian Innovation System Report* (2014). p. 64.

(14.) ICAA (2013). *20 Issues on Business Innovation,* p. 4. Retrieved November 2015 from http://www.charteredaccountants.com. au/.../20_Issues_Business%20Innovation

(15.) ICAA (2013). *20 Issues on Business Innovation,* p. 19.

(16.) ICAA (2013). *20 Issues on Business Innovation,* p. 23.

(17.) KPMG (2016). *Now or Never 2016 Global CEO Outlook.* Retrieved February 2017 from https://home.kpmg.com/ content/dam/kpmg/pdf/2016/06/2016-global-ceo-outlook. pdf

(18.) KPMG Australia (2016). *'Who dares wins' say Australian CEOs.* Retrieved February 2017 from https://home.kpmg.com/au/ en/home/media/press-releases/2016/06/who-dares-wins-say-australian-ceos-28-jun-2016.html

(19.) *Australian Innovation System Report* (2016). p. 4.

(20.) *Australian Innovation System Report* (2016). p. 4.

(21.) Martin Prosperity Institute (2015). *The Global Creativity Index 2015,* p14. Retrieved May 2017 from http://martinprosperity. org/media/Global-Creativity-Index-2015.pdf

(22.) Australian Government (2014). *Australian Innovation System Report,* p. 64. Retrieved November 2015 from http://industry. gov.au

(23.) http://www.mckinsey.com/business-functions/strategy-and-corporate-finance/our-insights/leadership-and-innovation

Chapter 7

(1.) Dictionary.com, Random House definition. *Failure.* Retrieved June 2017 from http://www.dictionary.com/browse/failure

(2.) Conner, T. (2016). *Creative activities promote day-to-day wellbeing: Otago research.* Retrieved June 2017 from http://www.otago.ac.nz/news/news/otago627504.html

Chapter 10

(1.)   Unilever (2017). *Open Innovation.* Retrieved June 2017 from https://www.unilever.com/about/innovation/ open-innovation/

(2.)   Business Victoria (2017). *Improving Innovation.* Retrieved June 2017 from http://www.business.vic.gov.au/marketing-sales-and-online/growth-innovation-and-measurement/ improving-business-innovation-and-examples

(3.)   Empathy Museum (2017). *Who we are.* Retrieved June 2017 from http://www.empathymuseum.com/#whoweare

(4.)   Stanford study: 'Give Your Ideas Some Legs: The Positive Effect of Walking on Creative Thinking'. Retrieved June 2017 from http://www.apa.org/pubs/journals/releases/xlm-a0036577.pdf

Chapter 11

(1.)   Wojcicki, S. (2011). *The Eight Pillars of Innovation.* Retrieved June 2017 from https://www.thinkwithgoogle.com/ marketing-resources/8-pillars-of-innovation/

(2.)   Hilbert, M. (2011). *The World's Technological Capacity to Store, Communicate, and Compute Information.* Retrieved June 2017 from http://www.uvm.edu/pdodds/files/papers/ others/2011/hilbert2011a.pdf

(3.)   James, J. (2016). *Data Never Sleeps 4.0.* Retrieved June 2017 from https://www.domo.com/blog/data-never-sleeps-4-0/

(4.)   NeoMam Studios (2017). *Thirteen Reasons Why Your Brain Craves Infographics.* Retrieved June 2017 from http:// neomam.com/interactive/13reasons/

(5.)   Changing Minds (2017). *Active Learning.* Retrieved June 2017 from http://changingminds.org/explanations/learning/ active_learning.htm

Chapter 12

(1.) Barsh, J., Capozzi, M., and Davidson, J. (2008). *Leadership and Innovation.* Retrieved June 2017 from http://www.mckinsey.com/business-functions/strategy-and-corporate-finance/our-insights/leadership-and-innovation

(2.) Carone, C. (2013). *Want to Inspire Innovation? Reward Risk Takers.* Retrieved June 2017 from http://www.forbes.com/sites/christacarone/2013/09/12/rewardrisktakers/

(3.) Arndt, M. (2006). *3M's Seven Pillars of Innovation.* Retrieved June 2017 from https://www.bloomberg.com/news/articles/2006-05-09/3ms-seven-pillars-of-innovation

(4.) I just know this stuff.

(5.) Petrone, P. (2015). *Google Found Out That Giving Its Employees Trips To Hawaii is Better Than $1M Awards.* Retrieved June 2017 from https://business.linkedin.com/talent-solutions/blog/2015/07/google-found-out-that-giving-its-employees-trips-to-hawaii-is-better-than-1m-awards

(6.) Tata Group (2012). *Celebrating innovation.* Retrieved June 2017 from http://www.tata.com/article/inside/xqkFEPUqPbE=/TLYVr3YPkMU=

To download your inspiration and photography
guide and other great extras, visit
www.simonbanks.com.au/bookbonus

www.ingramcontent.com/pod-product-compliance
Lightning Source LLC
Chambersburg PA
CBHW071347210326
41597CB00015B/1565